LAWFARE: THE WAR AGAINST FREE SPEECH

A FIRST AMENDMENT GUIDE FOR REPORTING
IN AN AGE OF ISLAMIST LAWFARE

Brooke Goldstein and Aaron Eitan Meyer

thewaragainstfreespeech.com

1

THE CENTER FOR SECURITY POLICY
1901 Pennsylvania Avenue, Suite 201 Washington, DC 20006
Phone: (202) 835-9077 Email: info@securefreedom.org

For more information, please see securefreedom.org

Book design by David Reaboi.

❝ When wise men refuse to mention disagreeable facts, foolish and stupid men will have their say more than ever."[1]

ZECHARIAH CHAFEE, JR.

❝ Speech is powerful. It can stir people to action, move them to tears of both joy and sorrow, and—as it did here—inflict great pain. On the facts before us, we cannot react to that pain by punishing the speaker. As a Nation we have chosen a different course—to protect even hurtful speech on public issues to ensure that we do not stifle public debate."[2]

CHIEF JUSTICE JOHN ROBERTS

---

1 Zechariah Chafee, Jr., Government and Mass Communications: A Report from the Commission on the Freedom of the Press 130 (Univ. of Chicago Press 1947).

2 Chief Justice John Roberts, SNYDER v. PHELPS ET AL., 562 U. S. 131 S. Ct. 1207, 1220 (March 2, 2011). NOTE: This case involved the picketing of funerals for American soldiers who fell in combat during operations in Iraq and Afghanistan. The defendants, the odious Westboro Baptist Church, engaged in a loud demonstration outside the funeral of Marine Lance Corporal Matthew Snyder in order to broadcast their controversial ideology, after which Cpl. Snyder's father filed suit against the church. Nevertheless, the Supreme Court ruled by an 8-1 majority that Westboro's actions in the particular funeral at issue were constitutionally protected despite being hurtful even though their contribution to public discourse is relatively negligible and is overwhelmingly – and rightfully – condemned across the American political spectrum.

ACKNOWLEDGEMENTS

The authors would like to thank the Center for Security Policy for publishing this work. The authors would also like to thank the following for their considerable assistance during the writing and editing process: Qanta Ahmed, Jeffrey Azarva, Christine Brim, Inbar Gal, David B. Harris, Andrew Harrod, Jacqueline Kline, Daniel Kurland, David Reaboi, Benjamin Ryberg, Stephen S. Schwartz, Mark W. Smith, Ann Snyder, Nathaniel Sugarman, James Taranto, Richard Thompson, and Adam Turner. The authors would also like to thank their parents: Laurie and Jerome Meyer, and Ellen and Norman Goldstein.

Brooke Goldstein would also like to extend her gratitude to Professors Eva Hanks, and Malvina Halberstam, who worked to instill a deep respect for the rule of law, the American Constitution and the inalienable rights to property and free speech.

4

PRAISE FOR
LAWFARE: THE WAR AGAINST FREE SPEECH

❝ Freedom of speech is under assault from a direction that the United States and the West generally rejected centuries ago. "Blasphemy," as some define it, may not be pretty, but the suppression of speech is profoundly ugly, not to mention dangerous to a free and open society. This book explains why."

> AMB. JOHN BOLTON served as the U.S. permanent representative to the United Nations from 2005 to 2006. Prior to that, he was under secretary of state for arms control and international security. He is a senior fellow at the American Enterprise Institute, and the author of Surrender Is Not An Option.

" Winning the war on terrorism requires an aggressive defense against 'lawfare'—the misuse of our civil legal system by terrorism's facilitators, propagandists and apologists. Aaron Meyer and Brooke Goldstein have produced an essential primer on 'lawfare' which policymakers at every level of government should read, and act on."

> New York State Assemblyman RORY LANCMAN is the author of the Freedom to Report Terrorism Act and the Libel Tourism Protection Act.

" Mr. Meyer and Ms. Goldstein have compiled an impressive arsenal of important information critical to helping journalists fight back against the lawfare being waged on the West by Militant Islamists."

> MARK W. SMITH, Esq. is the New York Times bestselling author of The Official Handbook of the Vast Right-Wing Conspiracy: The Arguments You Need to Defeat the Looney Left and Disrobed: The New Battle Plan to Break the Left's Stranglehold on the Courts. He is a partner at Smith Valliere PLLC.

" A useful guide to First Amendment law and a timely chronicle of Islamist efforts to suppress speech."

> JAMES TARANTO is Contributing Editor at The Wall Street Journal.

" Those of us who have been at the business end of lawfare—Islamism's latest heavy weapon against America and the Constitution—will regard this book as the leading treatment of radical Islam's new threat to freedom and national security. Meyer and Goldstein respond with a careful, authoritative and highly readable guide to the Silencing War. Pioneering scholars and practitioners in the lawfare field, they take us through its legal and policy ramifications, and offer Americans the practical, workable solutions needed to come to grips with this historic, subversive challenge."

> DAVID B. HARRIS is a Barrister and Solicitor, Director, International and Terrorist Intelligence Program, INSIG-NIS Strategic Research Inc., successful defendant in Canadian Council on American Islamic Relations (CAIR-CAN) v. Harris, an Islamic libel lawfare case.

" The money I could have saved if I only had this book ten years ago..."

> DOUGLAS MURRAY is Associate Director of the Henry Jackson Society.

" Meyer and Goldstein shine the light of public scrutiny on lawfare—a form of jihadist bullying that has gone too long unchallenged. But they do more than describe the threat—they detail ideas for fighting to protect our civil liberties, in America and around the world."

EZRA LEVANT is a Canadian lawyer, conservative political activist and media figure. He is the founder and former publisher of the Western Standard, hosts The Source on Canadian television's Sun News Network, and is the author of many books, including Shakedown: How Our Government Is Undermining Democracy In The Name Of Human Rights.

TABLE OF CONTENTS

DISCLAIMER

This book is an informative publication by the Center for Security Policy; it does not constitute legal advice, is not intended to serve as legal advice, should not be relied upon as legal advice, and does not substitute for the assistance of qualified counsel. The publication and distribution of this book does not create an attorney-client or other fiduciary relationship. If legal advice or expert assistance is needed, a competent legal professional should be contacted.

The Center for Security Policy is a non-profit, non-partisan national security organization that specializes in identifying policies, actions, and resource needs that are vital to American security and then ensures that such issues are the subject of both focused, principled examination and effective action by recognized policy experts, appropriate officials, opinion leaders, and the general public. For further information, please visit the Center at securefreedom.org.

" The Liberty of the Press is essential to the security of freedom in a state; it ought, therefore, to be inviolably preserved."

THE CONSTITUTION OF THE STATE OF MASSACHUSETTS, 1780

THE BILL OF RIGHTS OF THE STATE OF NEW HAMPSHIRE, 1784

" At the heart of the First Amendment is the recognition of the fundamental importance of the free flow of ideas and opinions on matters of public interest and concern."

CHIEF JUSTICE WILLIAM H. REHNQUIST,
HUSTLER MAGAZINE V. FALWELL [3]

Freedom of speech and the press are the foundations of a free society. However, any protection of these liberties would ring hollow if it did not include the right to speak and to write *critically* about the most important and controversial issues of our times. Today's hot button issues include terrorism, terror financing, Islam, the Islamist movement and related topics. Unfortunately, the free speech rights of authors, researchers, and journalists commenting on these subjects are increasingly under attack through both violent and non-violent means.

The Islamist[4] movement is that which seeks to impose tenets of Islam, and specifically Shariah (authoritative,

---

3 Hustler Magazine v. Falwell, 485 U.S. 46, 50 (1988). As a general note, when a court opinion is cited, it has several components: the names of the parties come first. The next section refers to the published report of the cases. Here, 485 is the volume of the U.S. reporter, which is a collection of U.S. Supreme Court rulings, while 46 is the page number on which the case begins. The second number, 50, refers to the specific page on which a quote appears. Finally, the year in parentheses is the year in which an opinion was handed down.

institutionalized Islamic law dating back to the 9th Century) as a legal, political, religious and judicial authority in both Muslim states and in the West. It has two wings—one violent and one technically legal, which can operate apart but often reinforce each other. While the violent arm attempts to silence speech by burning cars when Danish cartoons of Mohammed are published, by murdering filmmakers such as Theo Van Gogh on the streets of Amsterdam,[5] and by forcing authors such as Ayaan Hirsi Ali and Dr. Wafa Sultan into hiding in the U.S.,[6] the legal arm is skillfully maneuvering within Western legal systems, both here and abroad, to silence and punish speech critical of radicalized Islam, terrorism and their sources of financing. Over the last decade, a more subtle challenge has emerged in the form of "lawfare."[7]

---

4 The terms "Islamist" or "Islamism" are commonly used as a synonym for those who promote and impose the political-military-legal Shariah doctrines of Islam. It does not refer to Muslims who practice a personal, pietistic observance of Islam solely as a religion. In different contexts, Islamism is also referred to as "political Islam," "Islamic fundamentalism," "militant Islam," "Islamic supremacism," or "Shariah-adherent Islam" -- all dedicated to imposing and enforcing Shariah law on Muslims and, when possible, on non-Muslims. As examples in the United States, the Muslim Brotherhood and Jama'at-e Islami are two major Islamist networks with influence through a large number of affiliated organizations. At the international level, the Organization of Islamic Conference is organized Islamism with representatives from 56 Muslim-majority nations plus "Palestine." Generally, Islamists oppose Western legal systems protecting human rights and civil liberties, particularly when those liberties conflict with authoritative, institutionalized Shariah law.

5 Van Gogh was shot and stabbed by Mohammed Bouyeri in the early morning of November 2, 2004, shortly after making the film Submission, which was highly critical of Islam's treatment of women. Bouyeri left a note on Van Gogh's body that threatened Dutch politician Ayaan Hirsi Ali, who has required 24/7 security protection since, and sent an open letter to Dutch parliamentarian Geert Wilders as well, making threats on his life.

6 Dr. Sultan, a Syrian-American psychiatrist, has been subject to death threats since she criticized the course Islam has taken in a February 21, 2006 interview with Al Jazeera. Among other criticisms of Islam, Dr. Sultan said, "You have become a captive of the Books; you are the ones who have failed to rise with your humanity beyond the mentality of the Middle Ages . . . ." "Transcript Translation: al-Jazeera – The Opposite Direction (26/02/2006), available online at http://aqoul.com/images/wafa_sultan.pdf [Last accessed April 20, 2010]

7 in his influential 2001 essay, Law and Military Interventions: Preserving Humanitarian Values in 21st Conflicts, Major General Charles Dunlap defined lawfare as "the use of law as a weapon of war" or "a method of warfare where law is used as a means of realizing a military objective." Charles J. Dunlap, Jr., Law and Military Interventions: Preserving Humanitarian Values in 21st Century Conflicts, Working Paper 5 (Boston: Harvard Kennedy School, 2001), available at

Although not a new phenomenon, lawfare was brought to the attention of the modern world in an essay by Major General Charles Dunlap, of the U.S. Air Force Judge Advocate General Corps, defining it as "the use of the law as a weapon of war."[8] The definition has since been expanded to include the *wrongful* manipulation of the legal system to achieve strategic military or political ends.[9] Lawfare consists of the *negative* manipulation of international and national human rights laws to achieve purposes other than, or contrary to those for which they were originally enacted.[10]

The strategic end of Islamist lawfare is to further the goals of the Islamist movement, one of which is to abolish public discourse critical of Islam and punish anything deemed blasphemous of its prophet Mohammad. Another goal of Islamist lawfare is to impede the free flow of public information about the threat of Islamist terrorism thereby limiting our ability to understand and destroy it. In this way, Islamist lawfare takes the

---

http://www.ksg.harvard.edu/cchrp/Web%20Working%20Papers/Use%20of%20Force/Dunlap2 001.pdf. Dunlap elaborated further that, while lawfare can manifest in many forms, "the one ever more frequently embraced by U.S. opponents is a cynical manipulation of the rule of law and the humanitarian values it represents." Id.

8 Id.

9 Definition used by The Lawfare Project. The Lawfare Project, www.thelawfareproject.org (last visited Nov. 15, 2010).

10 Id. Lawfare, especially in the context of free speech, refers to the often malicious abuse of the law and judicial systems. It is separate and distinct from the use of the legal system to pursue justice. We emphasize wrongful because lawfare is an inherently negative undertaking and must be defined as such to have any real meaning. Otherwise, we risk diluting the phenomenon and feeding the inability to distinguish between what is the correct application of the law on the one hand and what is lawfare on the other. Because that is the essence of the issue here: how do we distinguish between a constructive, legitimate legal battle from that which is a counterproductive perversion of the law, the latter of which should be allocated no precedent? The delineation is not as simple as some may like to make it. The question is not 'Who is the target?' but 'What is the intention?' behind the legal action: Is it to pursue justice, to apply the law in the interests of freedom, democracy and the marketplace of ideas, or is the intent to undermine the very system of laws being manipulated?

form of a complementary legal campaign to terrorism and asymmetric warfare.

Islamist lawfare is often predatory, filed without a serious expectation of winning, and undertaken as a means to intimidate, demoralize and bankrupt defendants. Complaints range in their claims from administrative actions[11] to defamation to workplace harassment to Islamophobia, and have resulted in books being banned and pulped, in thousands of dollars worth of fines and in publishing houses and newspapers rejecting important works on counter-terrorism out of fear of being the next target. From filing frivolous and malicious libel and "hate speech" lawsuits to lobbying for the resurgence of national and international blasphemy laws, we have seen a steady and alarming increase in Islamist lawfare over the past ten years. The cumulative result of these lawsuits and the threat thereof has created a detrimental chilling effect on open public dialogue about issues of national security and public concern. This chilling effect stems from a collective fear[12] of being slapped with a lawsuit or being targeted

---

11 When the nonpartisan Clarion Fund released the film Obsession in 2008, the Council on American Islamic Relations filed a spurious complaint with the Federal Elections Commission ("FEC") alleging that the film, which analyzes the nexus between radicalized Islam and terrorism, constituted unlawful lobbying for Presidential candidate John McCain, because McCain (and President Barack Obama) declared terrorism to be a central national security policy issue. Goldstein filed a response to the FEC which argues that the DVD in question was not partisan, that CAIR completely failed to prove its contention by a showing of evidence, and that CAIR brought the complaint in order to silence a viewpoint of which it was critical. See Brooke M. Goldstein, The Legal Project's Response to the Federal Election Commission: Regarding CAIR's Complaint Against the "Obsession" DVD, The Legal Project (Nov. 15, 2008), http://www.legal-project.org/130/the-legal-projects-response-to-the-federal.

12 This institutionalized fear has extended to works of fiction, as in the case of the 2008 novel The Jewel of Medina, a story centering on Mohammed's child bride, Aisha. Random House reneged on publishing the book after a reviewer hysterically warned of a variety of repercussions including violent reactions from the Muslim community. After the British publishing house Gibson Square subsequently announced it would publish the novel, Gibson publisher Martin Rynja's London home was firebombed. Beaufort Books eventually published the book in the U.S., to mixed reviews. Beaufort published the book's sequel, The Sword of Medina, on October 15, 2009.

with violence for printing anything deemed offensive to Muslims—including satirical cartoons.[13]

Moreover, the chilling effect is cascading over all areas of public discourse regarding Islam; from academia and the government to the media and entertainment industry. (e.g., Yale University Press excising Mohammad cartoons from a forthcoming scholarly book on the topic[14]; NPR's report that the Ft. Hood shooter's superiors recognized danger but failed to act for fear of seeming biased against Islam[15]; Producers of *2012* sparing Muslim but not Christian landmarks from disaster scenes for fear of a condemnatory "fatwa.")[16]

Mahdi Bray, of the Muslim American Society Freedom Foundation, articulated the strategy explicitly in a 2009 radio broadcast: "we've got to be willing to spend our money in a court of law ... and not necessarily because we're going to look for money, but...to...make you spend your money."[17] The potency of the approach was highlighted on February 26, 2010 when a Danish newspaper, which was sued by a Saudi law firm allegedly on behalf of 94,923 descendants of Mohammad for republishing

---

13 On September 30, 2005, the Danish newspaper Jyllands-Posten published twelve editorial cartoons depicting Mohammed in response to concerns about self-censorship on matters of Islam. This publication, for which Jyllands-Posten would later fearfully apologize, was used as an excuse for violent demonstrations as well as physical and legal threats against the publication, including a demand by Osama bin Laden that the cartoonists be handed over to him for trial and punishment for their 'crime' of offending Muslims. The controversy over the cartoons has continued for over five years, and is more fully considered in Chapter 7. Perhaps the most recognizable such cartoon is the depiction of Mohammed with a bomb in his turban.

14 Peter Berkowitz, Academia Goes Silent on Free Speech, Wall St. J. (Oct. 17, 2009), ttp://online.wsj.com/article/SB10001424052748704107204574469111623490506.html.

15 Daniel Zwerdling, Hasan's Supervisor Warned Army in 2007, Nat'l Pub. Radio (Nov. 18, 2009), http://www.npr.org/templates/story/story.php?storyId=120540125.

16 Ben Child, Emmerich Reveals Fear of Fatwa Axed 2012 Scene, Guardian (Nov. 3, 2009), http://www.guardian.co.uk/film/2009/nov/03/roland-emmerich-2012-kaaba.

17 Daniel Pipes, Islamists in the Courtroom, Daniel Pipes (June 5, 2007), http://www.danielpipes.org/4612/islamists-in-the-courtroom.

one of the Mohammad cartoons, issued a formal apology.[18] The paper's sole purpose in rerunning the cartoon had been to join other Danish papers in a unified stand against intimidation of the press following the 2007 threats on the life of the cartoon's creator.[19] Curiously, the paper defied the physical threats, but bowed in the face of legal ones.

In the international arena, the Organization of Islamic Cooperation ("OIC") and several of its member states have embarked on a campaign at the United Nations to globally criminalize any speech that "defames" or "blasphemes" Islam or its religious figures. Included in its list of things to ban is anything deemed "Islamophobic"—a politically charged term that would most likely include legitimate research involving Islamic terrorism. Yet the simple fact remains, freedom of religion does not entail carte blanche freedom to practice your religion absent criticism.

The cornerstones of any liberal democracy are the rights to speak freely and to criticize religion or government openly. Freedom of speech is not an abstraction; America's founders recognized it as a crucial bulwark against repressive governance or institutions. They acknowledged free speech and as a natural right—applying to all people at all times—and that no government, lobby group or court may unjustly curtail its expression. Attempts to subvert it through Islamist lawfare run directly counter to the founding principles of the United States. Journalists exercising this right by publishing articles on national security are doing their part to ensure the continued security of the

---

18 Politiken Settles Mohammed Cartoon Issue, Politiken (Feb. 26, 2010), http://politiken.dk/newsinenglish/article911102.ece.

19 Back to the Drawing Board: Danish Muhammad Cartoonist Returns with New Work, Spiegel Online (Nov. 12, 2008), http://www.spiegel.de/international/europe/0,1518,589954,00.html.

United States and the freedom of its citizens, and must be protected.

It is hoped that the information contained herein will work to embolden authors and experts by outlining the legal framework within which they are entitled to operate. This book will demonstrate to those involved in researching or reporting on matters relating to terrorism, terror financing, militant Islam or Shariah their rights under U.S. law. Case examples of previous Islamist lawfare lawsuits, and how to avoid potential lawfare without self-censoring oneself, will be detailed herein, noting the relevant differences between United States and European Law, as well as the various jurisdictional issues posed by Internet publications.

As noted in the preliminary Disclaimer, this book is not, nor is it intended to be, a substitute for the advice of appropriate legal counsel. Nonetheless, it may prove an informative resource for those at risk of being targeted by Islamist lawfare against freedom of speech. For information on the phenomenon of lawfare in general, visit thelawfareproject.org.

1

THE LAW OF DEFAMATION IN
THE UNITED STATES

" Freedom of discussion, if it would fulfill its historic function in this nation, must embrace all issues about which information is needed or appropriate to enable the members of society to cope with the exigencies of their period."

JUSTICE FRANK MURPHY, THORNHILL V. ALABAMA[20]

In the wake of the September 11th, 2001 terrorist attacks, several media organizations published articles stating that the charity Global Relief Foundation was under federal investigation for alleged ties to terrorist organizations, and that the charity might have its assets frozen as a result. Global Relief Foundation filed a lawsuit against six media organizations and eight reporters, claiming that the articles were **defamatory**.[21]

---

20 310 U.S. 88, 102 (1940)
21 *Global Relief Found., Inc. v. New York Times Co.*, 390 F.3d 973 (7th Cir. 2004) Note: F.3d refers to reports of the federal Courts of Appeal. The notation in the parentheses means that the case was heard by the Seventh Circuit Court of Appeals, and the case was decided in 2004.

" Under the First Amendment there is no such thing as a false idea. However pernicious an opinion may seem, we depend for its correction not on the conscience of judges and juries but on the competition of other ideas. But there is no constitutional value in false statements of fact."

JUSTICE LEWIS F. POWELL, JR., GERTZ V. ROBERT WELCH, INC.[22]

Black's Law Dictionary defines **defamation** as "[t]he act of harming the reputation of another by making a false statement to a third person."[23]

In order for a plaintiff[24] to successfully bring a case for defamation against a defendant, the plaintiff must make an initial showing of six essential elements:

❶ A **FALSE** STATEMENT OF **FACT**:

The plaintiff must demonstrate that the statement at issue is both of a **factual** nature and **false**. If the defendant's statement cannot be proven to be false, it cannot serve as grounds for a defamation suit. Truth is an absolute defense to defamation.

EXAMPLE. "Leslie is a fool" is a statement of opinion, not of fact, and is not actionable as defamation.[25]

---

22 Gertz v. Robert Welch, Inc., 418 U.S. 323, 339-40 (1974).

23 Black's Law Dictionary 183 (2d ed. 2001).

24 A plaintiff is the person who brings the lawsuit, in this case claiming that he has been defamed, while the defendant is the party accused of having made the defamatory statement at issue.

25 For example, in Bauer v. Murphy, 191 Wis.2d 517 (1995), a college basketball player sued her coach for slander after being called "a disgrace," and the suit was dismissed by the court and by the Wisconsin Court of Appeal because mere name-calling is not actionable as defamation. See also

EXAMPLE. "John stole Bob's car." This is a statement that purports to relay a fact about John. If in fact, John did not steal Bob's car, if the statement is untrue, the statement may be judged defamatory. If, however, the statement is true, it may not be defamatory.

EXAMPLE. "X Foundation is under federal investigation for alleged ties to terrorism" is a statement that purports to relay a fact about X Foundation. If in fact, X Foundation is under investigation for the reasons stated, if the statement is true, the statement may not be defamatory. If the statement is false, if there is no investigation underway, the statement may be judged defamatory.

❷ THE STATEMENT MUST BE **OF OR CONCERNING** THE PLAINTIFF:

To prove defamation, the plaintiff must show that the statement at issue is about (of or concerning) the plaintiff himself, or herself, or itself.[26]

EXAMPLE. "All people with brown hair have committed crimes." This statement is non-actionable because it is not of or concerning a particular person.

EXAMPLE. "Ralph just robbed that liquor store." This statement, if false, may be used as the basis for a defamation claim by Ralph, since it is clearly about him.

In the United States, you cannot be successfully sued for defamation simply for disparaging a religion or ethnicity, since it does not meet the minimum requirement that the statement is "of

---

Bander v. Metropolitan Life Ins. Co., 313 Mass. 337 (1943).

26 In certain cases, corporations can sue for defamation, but the corporation must be able to show that the statement referred to it, either explicitly or by demonstrating that a reasonable person reading the statement would conclude that it was about the corporation.

or concerning" a *specific* individual. The issue of "group libel" will be considered explicitly in Chapter Four.

❸ THE STATEMENT MUST BE **PUBLISHED**:

This means that the statement must be communicated to a third person, someone other than the plaintiff, either verbally or in writing, electronically or by any other means of communication. EXAMPLE. If Carrie says to John, "John, I know you stole Bob's car," and no one is around to hear it other than John, the statement has not been published. If, on the other hand, Carrie says to Morton, "Hey Morton, I happen to know for a fact that John stole Bob's car," Carrie's statement about John is considered to be published (since it was said to someone other than John) and if false, may be judged defamatory.

❹ THE STATEMENT AT ISSUE MUST TEND TO **HARM** THE PLAINTIFF'S **REPUTATION**:

This means that an average person hearing or reading the statement would tend to view the plaintiff in a negative light as a result of the statement.[27]

❺ THE DEFENDANT MUST BE AT **FAULT** IN MAKING THE DEFAMATORY STATEMENT:

There are different standards of fault that are applied depending on the nature of the case. The element of fault will be covered in greater detail in Chapter Two.[28]

---

27 The highly influential legal treatise The Restatement (Second) of Torts § 559 (1977) defines harm to one's reputation as that which would "lower him in the estimation of the community or to deter third persons from associating or dealing with him."

28 See generally Philadelphia Newspapers v. Hepps, 418 U.S. 767 (1986).

❻ THE PLAINTIFF MUST SUFFER DAMAGES AS A RESULT OF THE STATEMENT:

In defamation suits for libel (for the definition of libel see p. 26), the court will presume damages. That is to say that the court will not demand the plaintiff demonstrate specific monetary damage has occurred. In slander cases on the other hand (for the definition of slander see 26), the plaintiff must show that he or she has suffered actual monetary damage as a result of the defamatory statement being published.

NOTE: Because statements are presumed to be true in the United States until proven otherwise, due process requires that the plaintiff shoulder the burden of giving the court evidence establishing the six elements above. If the plaintiff fails to do so, the defendant will not be held liable. This is not the case, however, in all Western democracies. In England, for example, the burden of proof rests upon the defendant.[29]

IN SUM: In order for a plaintiff to successfully proceed with a defamation lawsuit against a defendant in the United States, the plaintiff must fulfill the burden of demonstrating to the court, that defendant's statement was (i) *about* him/her/it, (ii) *published*, (iii) *harmed* his/her/its reputation and (iv) is *false*, and that the plaintiff suffered (v) *damages* as a result of defendant's (vi) *fault*.

---

29 In England and Wales, plaintiffs (or "claimants") are presumed to have good reputations. Therefore, allegedly defamatory statements are considered false unless a defendant can prove the truth of the statement. This is precisely the opposite of U.S. law, which presumes that statements are true until proven false, hence the essence of being "innocent until proven guilty" of defamation, to borrow an expression from criminal law.

Defamation can take two different forms:

❶ LIBEL

Generally, if the statement at issue is in a *fixed and permanent form*, a defamation suit will involve a question of libel. Libel lawsuits are much more common than slander, and include anything written or recorded (including recordings of the spoken word) [30], posted on the Internet, published in books, newspapers, journals and so on.

❷ SLANDER

Statements that are transitory in nature, which are neither fixed nor permanent in form, are categorized as slander. This traditionally includes spoken statements and gestures when they are not recorded in a fixed and permanent form. For example, if you stand on a street corner and yell something and nobody is filming or recording you, your spoken word may be considered slander, but if you write down the same words and publish it as an Opinion-Editorial, or if you were being filmed and the video is uploaded onto the Internet, the speech may be considered libel.

NOTE: The difference between libel and slander is very important when it comes to proving damages. As alluded to previously, in order to win a case for slander, you must be able to show actual

---

30 Technological progress has moved broadcasts into the libel category since they are now routinely recorded and in many cases posted to the Internet, thus rendering the broadcasts permanently accessible in fixed and tangible form.

pecuniary (monetary) damages.[31] On the other hand, when a plaintiff initiates a libel suit, the court will presume damages.

Now that defamation has been defined, there are several general tips that journalists should keep in mind.

❶ TRUTH

Under U.S. law, the **truth** is an absolute defense to defamation. That is, *if your statement is true* you can never be found liable for defamation in the United States. Always make sure that you have evidence to support your conclusions of fact, including written records, footnotes, and reliable sources. If you publish a statement you reasonably believe to be true based on your research, however, you may be protected even if the statement is later shown to be false. The reasoning for this protection was set forth by the U.S. Supreme Court, which stated:

> That erroneous statement is inevitable in free debate, and that it must be protected if the freedoms of expression are to have the 'breathing space' that they 'need . . . to survive[.]'[32]

How does the defense of truth work? Recall the Global Relief Foundation (GRF) case mentioned at the beginning of this chapter, in which GRF sued several media publications and reporters after they published articles stating that GRF was under federal investigation for alleged ties to terrorist organizations, and

---

31 There was a historical exception to this rule called slander per se that was treated much like libel cases in that statements involving certain allegations were considered so damaging as to not require proof of said damage. This subcategory of slander was effectively eliminated by the Supreme Court ruling in Gertz. v. Robert Welch, Inc., in which the Court reversed a lower court ruling partly due to the fact that the trial jury "was permitted to presume damages without proof of injury," Gertz v. Robert Welch, 418 U.S. 323, 352 (1974).

32 N.Y. Times Co. v. Sullivan, 376 U.S. 254, 271-72 (1964), citing NAACP v. Button, 371 U.S. 415, 433 (1963).

that the charity might have its assets frozen as a result. While the case was underway, the United States Treasury Department officially named GRF as a Specially Designated Global Terrorist, which substantiated what the newspapers had published, since GRF was indeed investigated, and subsequently had its assets frozen because of the investigation's findings. The defendant media corporations and journalists then moved for the judge to dismiss the case, since their statements were shown by the government to be substantially **true**.[33] The Global Relief Foundation appealed to a higher court, but the Seventh Circuit Court of Appeals upheld the dismissal.[34] Note that, in this case, even though the truth of the matter alleged was proven *after* the statement was made, defendants did not need to prove that their allegations were true at that time they made them. Rather, the Court found it sufficient that "The fact of the investigation was true whether or not it was publicly known. That is all that the defendants need to show for the defense of substantial truth. This they have done."[35]

Note that when reporting on the statement of another, it may be necessary to prove the truth that underlies the statement, not merely the fact that someone said it, even if the report is accurate. For example, say a journalist wrote "Susan said that 'Ralph was arrested for robbing a liquor store.'" This statement can leave the journalist open to a libel suit by Ralph based on the author's report of what Susan said, even if the journalist published Susan's statement verbatim, but *only* if Ralph was not in fact

33 Global Relief Found., Inc. v. N.Y. Times Co., 2003 U.S. Dist. LEXIS 2465, 6 (N.D. Ill. Feb. 19, 2003) (the abbreviation N.D. Ill denotes that this case was heard by the federal Northern District of Illinois).

34 Global Relief Found., Inc. v. N.Y. Times Co., 390 F.3d 973 (7th Cir. 2004).

35 Id. at 989

arrested for robbing a liquor store (that is, only if Susan's statement is false.) While there are additional defenses available in this type of scenario, it illustrates the need for a journalist to perform due diligence in investigating one's facts – regardless of the origin of the statement.

❷ REASONABLE RELIANCE ON EXPERTS

Oftentimes as a journalist, you're relying on the expertise of others. For example, if you plan to publish an article on Company X polluting the environment, or funding a terrorist group, you would have to rely on the conclusions drawn by experts in the field. Are you allowed to incorporate these statements into an article without being qualified to judge the underlying truth or validity of the statements? The general answer is yes if you reasonably relied on the expertise of others.[36]

EXAMPLE. A journalist publishes an article about government investigations into Person Y's bank account. The article includes a quote from a widely recognized expert on terror-financing obtained during an interview and alleging that "Person Y set up the bank account to funnel money to terrorist groups." If the article presents an accurate, disinterested and objective account of the story, and if the journalist is deemed to have reasonably relied on the interviewee's expertise, a judge may hold the journalist's speech protected even if the expert's statement proves false.

There is a similar privilege in many jurisdictions known as the "wire service" defense, which protects those who republish

---

36 For example, a federal court in New York held that there is "a general republication defense applicable to anyone who republishes material from any source." Jewell v. NYP Holdings, Inc., 23 F.Supp.2d 348, 371 (S.D.N.Y. 1998). That court cited an earlier decision by the New York Court of Appeals, the highest court in the state, which had held that "a publisher is entitled to rely on the research of an established writer," in a case that involved the use of "an experienced researcher." Weiner v. Doubleday & Co., 74 N.Y.2d 586, 595-96 (1989).

statements from reliable publications, so long as the re-publisher has no substantial reason to doubt the accuracy of the original article's author.[37] So it's safe to say that if you rely on a well-known expert or republish a statement from a recognized authority on the subject with no reason to doubt its veracity, you have acted within your rights as a journalist. It is always important to do your research, however; try not to rely on only one source, and always save your research in case you ever need to build the case as to why you were acting reasonably.

For example, consider the case of several newspapers that were sued by security guard Richard Jewell. Jewell was a security guard working at Olympic Park in Atlanta for the 1996 Olympic Games, when he discovered a bomb. Initially lauded as a hero, he was wrongly accused of being the bomber after several newspapers ran stories accusing him on the basis of uncorroborated information, including the *Atlanta-Journal Constitution* (AJC), which ran a front-page story highlighting Jewell as the subject of an investigation and implying that he was guilty. Jewell sued the newspapers for libel, and with the exception of AJC[38], each defendant settled with Jewell. By the time of his death in 2007, Jewell's name had become "shorthand for a person accused of wrongdoing in the media based on scanty information."[39]

---

37 This defense was first established by the Florida Supreme Court in the case Layne v. Tribune Co., 108 Fla. 177 (1933), and later adopted by other jurisdictions. Note: whenever a citation refers to a state, the reference is to a ruling from the state's highest court, in this case that of Florida. Case law may differ from state to state, and readers are strongly encouraged to consult with an attorney to determine the applicable law in their jurisdiction(s).

38 See page 43.

39 Harry R. Weber, Former Olympic Park Guard Jewell Dies, Wash. Post (Aug. 30, 2007), available at http://www.washingtonpost.com/wp-dyn/content/article/2007/08/30/AR2007083000324.html.

❸ REPORTING ON GOVERNMENT REPORTS
(THE "FAIR REPORTING PRIVILEGE")

Wherever possible, quote directly from a governmental report or judicial ruling itself. By doing so, you may be protected by the "fair reporting" privilege, though the extent of its protection varies from jurisdiction to jurisdiction. Generally, the privilege protects reporters who republish or report on court proceedings or government-issued documents when the report is "accurate and fair." In Florida, for example, "The news media has been given a qualified privilege to accurately report on the information they receive from government officials."[40] The privilege applies when the report is a **fair and accurate** account of what occurred during **official proceedings** (e.g. a court hearing, or a meeting of a public body).

❹ ACCURACY

Despite the protection of "substantial truth," being **accurate** can still mean the difference between winning and losing a defamation case, as the following example demonstrates.

In a case found in many law school textbooks, a disabled veteran of World War II wrote an essay for a class in which he accused the commanding officer of a depot camp of "*knowingly permitting*" a series "of cruel, unusual and unauthorized punishment upon prisoners." On the other hand, a footnote at the end of the article stated that the officer had been found guilty by a military court "of permitting cruel and unusual punishment of American soldiers." In fact, the officer had been acquitted of "knowingly permitting" these punishments, and was only found

---

40 Woodard v. Sunbeam Television Corp., 616 So.2d 501, 502 (Fla. 3d Dist. Ct. App. 1993), citing Ortega v. Post-Newsweek Stations, Fla., Inc., 510 So. 2d 972 (Fla. 3d Dist. Ct. App. 1987), rev. denied, 518 So. 2d 1277 (Fla. 1987)

guilty of the much lesser charge of "permitting" them. The officer sued the disabled veteran and the publisher of the book in which the essay appeared for libel, and when the case reached the Pennsylvania Supreme Court, the court held that the difference between being found guilty of "knowingly permitting" and merely "permitting" the punishments meant that the article was *not* substantially true and therefore defamatory.[41] Had the author been more accurate and omitted the word "knowingly," the outcome of the case would have been different.

What this means for journalists writing about terrorism and terror finance in particular is that it is extremely important to be precise and specific when reporting on government investigations, official reports, legal procedures and their outcomes. For example, Chapter 113B of the United States Code contains several statutes that impose federal penalties for assisting terrorism, with different provisions depending on whether one is "harboring or concealing terrorists,"[42] "providing material support to terrorists"[43] or to "designated foreign terrorist organizations,"[44] financing terrorism,[45] "or receiving military-type training from a foreign terrorist organization."[46] When reporting, get it right! Accuracy is key.

In a similar vein, even when you're relying on a source in good faith, be certain that your source is reliable, despite additional protections for media defendants that will be addressed in Chapter Two. Corroborating evidence and maintaining

41 Kilian v. Doubleday & Co., Inc., 367 Pa. 117 (1951).

42 18 U.S.C. § 2339 (1996). This citation refers to Title 18 of the United States Code, the federal civil and penal code, section 2339.

43 18 U.S.C. § 2339A (1996).

44 18 U.S.C. § 2339B (1996).

45 18 U.S.C. § 2339C (1996).

46 18 U.S.C. § 2339D (1996).

complete and accurate records will help ensure that you can protect yourself against any allegations of fault later on.

2

CONSTITUTIONAL REQUIREMENTS & PROTECTIONS FOR THE PRESS

❝ The First Amendment presupposes that the freedom to speak one's mind is not only an aspect of individual liberty—and thus a good unto itself—but also is essential to the common quest for truth and the vitality of society as a whole.❞

JUSTICE JOHN PAUL STEVENS,
BOSE CORP. v. CONSUMERS UNION OF UNITED STATES, INC.[47]

❝ Of that freedom [that is, freedom of speech] one may say that it is the matrix, the indispensable condition, of nearly every other form of freedom.❞

JUSTICE BENJAMIN N. CARDOZO,
PALKO v. CONNECTICUT[48]

---

47 Bose Corp. v. Consumers Union of U.S., Inc., 466 U.S. 485, 503-04 (1984).

48 Palko v. Connecticut, 302 U.S. 319, 327 (1937).

Even before the United States Constitution was ratified in 1789, the crucial role of the press in fostering discourse on matters of public concern was not only recognized, but hallowed. In 1776, the newly declared state of North Carolina's constitution declared, "That the freedom of the press is one of the great bulwarks of liberty, and therefore ought never to be restrained."[49]

The unparalleled recognition of the pivotal role played by the press has led to a series of U.S. Supreme Court rulings that protect the press when reporting on public figures and matters of public concern. Beginning with the seminal case *New York Times Co. v. Sullivan*,[50] the Supreme Court has outlined three situations in which plaintiffs alleging defamation must meet additional requirements imposed by the Constitution. The situations are as follows: 1) when the plaintiff is a **public official**, 2) when the plaintiff is a **public figure**, or 3) when the subject matter of the article is an **issue of public concern**.

THE NEW YORK TIMES CASE AND PUBLIC OFFICIALS

During the struggle to end segregation, the *New York Times* newspaper published a full-page advertisement that described mistreatment of African-American student protestors at the hands of the city of Montgomery, Alabama. Montgomery Police Commissioner L.B. Sullivan sued[51] the *Times* for libel *even though Sullivan was not referred to by name or title in the advertisement.*[52] After the case went up to (and was decided by) the Alabama Supreme Court, the U.S. Supreme Court chose to hear it.

---

49 Id at 256.

50 N.Y. Times Co. v. Sullivan, 376 U.S. 254 (1964).

51 Id.

52 As mentioned in Chapter 1, an essential component to bringing a defamation case is that the

In its ruling, the U.S. Supreme Court overruled the Alabama state libel statute, establishing that under the U.S. Constitution, "[a] rule compelling the critic of official conduct to guarantee the truth of all his factual assertions—and to do so on pain of libel judgments virtually unlimited in amount—l eads to ... 'self-censorship.'"[53] Moreover, the Court held, "Under such a rule, would-be critics of official conduct may be deterred from voicing their criticism, even though it is believed to be true and even though it is in fact true, because of doubt whether it can be proved in court or fear of the expense of having to do so."[54]

So, in the hope of forestalling self-censorship, the Supreme Court held that "constitutional guarantees require, we think, a federal rule that prohibits a public official from recovering damages for a defamatory falsehood relating to his official conduct unless he proves that the statement was made with actual malice—that is, with knowledge that it was false or with reckless disregard of whether it was false or not."[55] Following this case, the actual malice standard was established for all persons reporting on public officials and public figures as well as private plaintiffs seeking punitive damages for reports on matters of public concern. *The rule holds that in order to be found liable for defamation of a public official or figure, the plaintiff must prove the defendant acted with actual malice or reckless disregard for the truth of the matter*

---

statement at issue is "of and concerning" the plaintiff. In this case, the Court found that the libel count could not possibly succeed because the statement was not "of and concerning" the plaintiff. Sullivan unsuccessfully attempted to argue that, as he supervised the Montgomery police department, a reference in the advertisement to "police" meant he himself. Nevertheless, we mention this case in order to illustrate the actual malice standard when the statement at issue concerns a public figure.

53 376 U.S. at 279.

54 Id.

55 Id. at 279-280.

asserted. The same is true for a statement concerning an issue of public concern.

The term **actual malice** is extremely important, since it is the applicable standard for journalists writing about public officials, public figures, or issues of public concern. In such cases, the plaintiff bears the considerable burden of proving actual malice with "convincing clarity."[56]

Actual malice entails either (i) publishing a statement regardless of the fact that you **know it is false**, or (ii) publishing with a **reckless disregard** for the truth of the matters asserted.

The Supreme Court has described the actual malice test deeming "only those false statements **made with the high degree of awareness of their probable falsity demanded by the *New York Times*...**may be the subject of either civil or criminal sanctions."[57] 'Criminal libel' is a dying concept in the United States, and will not be considered in this book for that reason.[58]

Reckless disregard is a subjective standard that requires a showing that the defendant entertained **serious doubts** as to the veracity of the information, and published it regardless.[59] Mere failure to investigate, or general carelessness, though not recommended, does not meet the legal standard for reckless disregard. Keeping track of investigative research and corroborating sources is of invaluable assistance in preventing a claim of reckless disregard.

---

56 Id. at 285-86.
57 Garrison v. Louisiana, 379 U.S. 64, 74 (1964).
58 Id. at 68-69
59 St. Amant v. Thompson, 390 U.S. 727 (1968).

IN SUMMARY: If a defendant is sued for writing about a public official, public figure or on an issue of public concern, the plaintiff will only succeed if s/he can demonstrate to the court, with convincing clarity, that the defendant either (i) knew the statement to be false, (ii) published the statement with a high degree of awareness that the statement was likely false, or (iii) published the statement regardless of the fact that s/he has serious doubts as to its truth.

WHO IS A PUBLIC OFFICIAL?

The *New York Times* case dealt with City Commissioners, but the precise definition of who is a public official did not come about until 1966, when the U.S. Supreme Court defined public officials as "at the very least ... those among the hierarchy of government employees who have, or appear to the public to have, substantial responsibility for or control over the conduct of governmental affairs."[60] Five years later, the Supreme Court extended the definition to cover candidates for public office, *regardless of whether the candidate was thereafter elected or not,* when it ruled against Alphonse Roy, who had unsuccessfully run in the New Hampshire Democratic Party's 1960 Senate primary elections and who sued a local newspaper for describing him as "a former small-time bootlegger."[61] Public officials therefore may include members of the government such as members of Congress, elected officials, appointed officials, or government employees that exert substantial control over the affairs of their department. Keep in mind however, that different jurisdictions

---

60 Rosenblatt v. Baer, 383 U.S. 75, 85 (1966).
61 Monitor Patriot Co. v. Roy, 401 U.S. 265 (1971).

define a "public official" differently so it is necessary to consult with an attorney familiar with local applicable law.

WHO IS A PUBLIC FIGURE?

The rationale underlying the unparalleled protections afforded free speech in the United States has always been to foster free and open discourse on matters of public concern. Public figures alleging defamation have been held to the same higher standard as public officials, on the basis that they command "a substantial amount of independent public interest" and have the means to publicly refute defamatory statements without resorting to lawsuits.[62] As Supreme Court Chief Justice Earl Warren put it, the *New York Times* standard extends to individuals who are "intimately involved in the resolution of important public questions or, by reason of their fame, shape events in areas of concern to society at large."[63] Supreme Court Justice Powell further explained that "[i]n some instances an individual may achieve such pervasive fame or notoriety that he becomes a public figure for all purposes and in all contexts. More commonly, an individual voluntarily injects himself or is drawn into a particular public controversy, and thereby becomes a public figure for a limited range of issues."[64]

As alluded to in the quote above, there are two kinds of public figures, **universal** public figures, and **limited** public figures. A **universal** public figure is someone who is always in the public spotlight (like a well-known actor or musician), while a **limited** public figure may only have this status in regard to a particular matter, such as "**purposeful activity** amounting to a thrusting of

---

62 Curtis Publ'g Co. v. Butts, 388 U.S. 130, 155 (1967).
63 Id. at 164 (Warren, J., concurring).
64 Gertz. v. Robert Welch, Inc., 418 U.S. 323, 345 (1974).

his personality into the 'vortex' of an important public controversy."[65] While the Supreme Court has never formulated a specific test to determine who is a public figure, otherwise private figures will not be considered "public" without voluntarily, affirmatively thrusting themselves into the limelight to some degree. To illustrate, in a libel case stemming from the highly public divorce of Mary Alice and Russell Firestone,[66] the U.S. Supreme Court noted that,

> [W]hile participants in some litigation may be legitimate "public figures," either generally or for the limited purpose of that litigation, the majority will more likely resemble respondent [Mary Alice Firestone], drawn into a public forum largely against their will in order to attempt to obtain the only redress available to them or to defend themselves against actions brought by the State or by others.[67]

Drawing the line between a limited public figure and a private figure is complex, yet there are several general principles to bear in mind when determining whether the subject of an article might, him or herself, be deemed a **limited public figure** in the eyes of the law:

LIMITED PUBLIC FIGURE: In order for an otherwise private individual to be considered a limited public figure, there must exist more than mere public interest in that person, but an actual public *controversy* surrounding the person. If the person has **voluntarily** thrust him- or herself into the public spotlight, then he is probably a limited public figure. Consider the *Firestone* case just mentioned,

---

65 388 U.S. at 155.
66 Russell Firestone was the heir of the Firestone and Tire Rubber Company; however, Mary Alice was not famous in any way other than her marriage to Russell and the contentious nature of their divorce.
67 Time Inc. v. Firestone, 424 U.S. 448, 457 (1976).

in which an extremely messy public divorce was not sufficient to raise Mary Alice Firestone to the level of public figure, even though it was widely covered by the media. As the Supreme Court noted, she "did not assume any role of especial prominence in the affairs of society, other than perhaps Palm Beach society, *and she did not thrust herself to the forefront of any particular public controversy in order to influence the resolution of the issues involved in it.*"[68] [Emphasis added]

The determination of whether a person can be considered a **voluntary limited public figure** for the purpose of a defamation claim, tends to hinge on the answers to the following six questions:

* Has the plaintiff voluntarily injected him/herself into the public spotlight or voluntarily assumed a role of special prominence in a public controversy?

* Has the plaintiff sought to influence the outcome of the controversy through the press?

* Did the controversy exist prior to the publication of the defamatory statement?

* Did the plaintiff retain public figure status at the time of the statement's publication?

* Does the plaintiff have access to effective channels of mass-communication?

* Is the plaintiff able to refute or correct the allegedly defamatory statement without resorting to a lawsuit?

If the answer to several of the above is in the affirmative, it is more likely than not that an otherwise private person will be forced to prove the additional burden of actual malice in order to recover for defamation, since the court will consider him a voluntarily public figure in regard to the case at bar.

---

68 Id.

Note also, that the subject of an article may still be a **voluntary public figure**, if the person could have reasonably foreseen that his or her conduct would lead to a matter of **public concern,** and continued regardless. Thus, in his dissent in the *Firestone* case, the late Justice Thurgood Marshall criticized the majority for underestimating "the degree to which Mrs. Firestone can be said to have voluntarily acted in a manner that invited public attention."[69]

A more recent example of a **voluntary limited public figure** would be Richard Jewell, the security guard mentioned in Chapter One. His libel suit against the *Atlanta-Journal Constitution* after the paper ran a front-page story highlighting that he was the subject of an investigation stretched out over a decade, and remained undecided at the time of his death in 2007. A Georgia state trial court held that Jewell was a voluntary limited public figure under a three-part test set forth by the 11th Circuit Court of Appeals,[70] and Jewell appealed. The appellate court explained that, in Jewell's case, "[u]nder this test, the court must isolate the public controversy, examine the plaintiff's involvement in the controversy, and determine whether the alleged defamation was germane to the plaintiff's participation in the controversy. Whether a person is a public figure, general or limited, is a question of law for the court to resolve."[71] The court affirmed the trial court's ruling that Jewell was a limited public figure, and therefore had to prove "by clear and convincing evidence ... actual malice on the part of the defendant."[72]

---

69 Id. at 487

70 Silvester v. American Broadcasting Cos., Inc., 839 F.2d 1491, 1494 (11th Cir. 1988)

71 Atlanta Journal-Constitution v. Jewell, 251 Ga. App. 808, 817 (Ga. Ct. App. 2001). The Georgia Supreme Court and the U.S. Supreme Court both declined to grant certiorari, allowing this judgment to stand.

72 Id. at 823.

The primary factor in the court's decision was the "extensive media coverage Jewell received"[73] and that he had "voluntarily assumed a position of influence in the controversy."[74] In particular, "Jewell granted ten interviews and one photo shoot in the three days between the bombing and the reopening of the park, mostly to prominent members of the national press... Jewell's participation in the public discussion of the bombing exceeds what has been deemed sufficient to render other citizens public figures"[75]

By contrast, consider the case of *Gertz v. Welch*, in which a magazine called *American Opinion* published an article about a Chicago police officer who had been convicted of murder in the second degree for shooting a youth named Nelson.[76] The article claimed that the officer's prosecution and conviction were a frame-up, and was part of a Communist conspiracy against the police. This article also took aim at the attorney hired by the deceased youth's family to represent them in a civil trial, Elmer Gertz, accusing him of being a Leninist, and member of several Communist or socialist organizations. Gertz sued the magazine's publisher for defamation over what were false allegations, and the case eventually reached the Supreme Court, which found that Gertz had not placed himself in the public spotlight, was therefore a private figure, and did not have to prove the magazine acted with actual malice in publishing the article about him. In other words, despite the fact that the shooting and the controversy surrounding it *were* issues of public concern, Gertz did not automatically turn into a public figure by mere virtue of representing his client.

---

73 Id. at 818.
74 Id.
75 Id.
76 418 U.S. 323 (1974).

According to the court, even though Gertz served as an officer of local civic groups and of various professional organizations, had published several books and articles on legal subjects, and "was consequently well known in some circles, he had achieved no general fame or notoriety in the community."[77] Consequently, the court allowed Gertz to argue his claim without requiring him to meet a higher burden of proof. As the *Gertz* Court explained:

> The first remedy of any victim of defamation is self-help -- using available opportunities to contradict the lie or correct the error and thereby to minimize its adverse impact on reputation. Public officials and public figures usually enjoy significantly greater access to the channels of effective communication and hence have a more realistic opportunity to counteract false statements than private individuals normally enjoy. Private individuals are therefore more vulnerable to injury, and the state interest in protecting them is correspondingly greater.[78]

WHAT IS AN ISSUE OF PUBLIC CONCERN?

When a matter of "public concern" or a "public controversy" is at issue in a defamation case, the plaintiff must fulfill additional constitutional requirements in order to win. Specifically, when there is a matter of public concern at issue, and the plaintiff is a public figure, the plaintiff must show actual malice. On the other hand, if the Court finds that the plaintiff is a private figure who has some tangential connection to a public issue, he or she does not have to prove actual malice, but still has to prove that the defendant acted with 'gross irresponsibility.' As explained

---

77 Id. at 351-52

78 Id.

previously, if an attorney were to represent an accused terrorist, the attorney does **not** necessarily become a public figure, though the matter of the trial itself **is** of public concern and the attorney's **client** may indeed him/herself be considered a limited public figure. If the attorney is considered a private figure, s/he would not have to show actual malice to recover damages, but would need to prove that the defendant acted in a grossly irresponsible fashion in researching, writing and publishing the statement at issue. Gross irresponsibility can be considered one step below the actual malice standard.

In *Chapadeau v. Utica Observer-Dispatch, Inc.*, the New York Court of Appeals held that a school teacher (a private figure) who was incorrectly included in a newspaper article about arrests for heroin usage (a matter of public concern) had to "establish, by a preponderance of the evidence, that the publisher acted in a grossly irresponsible manner without due consideration for the standards of information gathering and dissemination ordinarily followed by responsible parties."[79] The Court of Appeals held that Chapadeau was not able to prove 'gross irresponsibility' on the part of the newspaper, and affirmed the lower court's dismissal of Chapadeau's libel suit.

Precise definitions regarding the outer limits of public concern may differ from state to state. The highest court in New York State has held that the determination as to whether a matter is of public concern is up to the press. "Absent clear abuse, the courts will not second-guess editorial decisions as to what constitutes matters of genuine public concern."[80] Despite this level of deference, it is best not to assume that a court will agree that an

---

79 Chapadeau v. Utica Observer-Dispatch, Inc., 38 N.Y.2d 196, 199 (1975).
80 Huggins v. Moore, 94 N.Y.2d 296, 303 (1999).

issue is one of public concern. The Court in the *Chapadeau* case held that "the arrest of a public school teacher for unlawful possession of a hypodermic needle and felony possession of heroin" meant that "the challenged communication falls within the sphere of legitimate public concern."[81] As in most things, blindly assuming that an issue is one of public concern just because it was a focus of media attention, could prove a major mistake.

IN SUMMARY: When you have an issue of public concern and a public plaintiff, the actual malice standard must be met by the plaintiff to recover. With an issue of public concern and a private plaintiff, the gross negligence standard applies. Whether or not there exists an issue of public concern comes into play when (1) considering whether an otherwise private person can be turned into a public plaintiff, necessitating s/he prove actual malice (this may only occur if the otherwise private plaintiff thrust him/herself voluntarily into the public spotlight) and (2) when a private plaintiff sues a private defendant, the latter writing about an issue of public concern, which will necessitate the plaintiff showing gross irresponsibility on behalf of the defendant.

WHO IS A MEDIA DEFENDANT?

There is a quote at the beginning of this book, stating that "the Liberty of the Press is essential to the security of freedom in a state; it ought, therefore, to be inviolably preserved."[82] Similarly, the North Carolina state constitution declared in 1776, "that the freedom of the press is one of the great bulwarks of liberty, and therefore ought never to be restrained."

---

81 38 N.Y.2d at 200.

82 The text is identical in both the Constitution of the State of Massachusetts, 1780 and The Bill of Rights of the State of New Hampshire, 1784.

Given the importance of freedom of the press in American history, it is unsurprising that the course of American legal development has led to considerable protections being created expressly for members of the media. For example, the U.S. Supreme Court has held that "at least where a newspaper publishes speech of public concern, a private-figure plaintiff cannot recover damages without also showing that the statements at issue are false."[83]

In the age of mass media and the Internet, it can be difficult to determine who is a member of the media for libel defense purposes. As the following case demonstrates, this determination may be crucial.

Joe Kaufman is an investigative reporter and the chairman of Americans Against Hate, an institution created to combat bigotry, particularly as articulated through Shariah-adherent Islamism. In late 2007, Kaufman was sued by seven Texas-area Islamic organizations after writing an article that alerted readers to an event being held at Six Flags Over Texas, which Kaufman referred to as "Fanatic Muslim Family Day"[84] due to the event's sponsorship by the Islamic Circle of North America (ICNA), which Kaufman claimed to be "a radical Muslim organization that has physical ties with the Muslim Brotherhood and financial ties to Hamas."[85] Kaufman also mentioned the event's other main sponsor, the Islamic Association of North Texas (IANT), and organized a lawful and peaceful protest outside the theme park on the day of the event.

---

83 Philadelphia Newspapers, Inc. v. Hepps, 475 U.S. 767, 768-69 (1986).

84 Joe Kaufman, Fanatic Muslim Family Day, FrontPage Mag., Sept. 28, 2007, http://archive.frontpagemag.com/readArticle.aspx?ARTID=28292.

85 As reprinted by the Texas Court of Appeals ruling in Kaufman v. Islamic Soc'y of Arlington, 291 S.W.3d 130 (Tex. Ct. App. 2009).

In response, seven separate and distinct Dallas-area Islamic organizations[86] that participated in the event but were *not mentioned* in Kaufman's article, filed a defamation suit against Kaufman. Kaufman then made use of a legal device called an interlocutory appeal. The interlocutory appeal allowed the appellate court to hear Kaufman's motion to dismiss the case before the trial judge rendered a final verdict. Kaufman was able to go forward with his appeal due to a Texas statute[87] which allows **media defendants** to take advantage of its expedience. The Texas statute defines media defendants to include:

> (M)ember[s] of the electronic or print media, acting in such capacity, or a person whose communication appears in or is published by the electronic or print media, arising under the free speech or free press clause of the First Amendment to the United States Constitution, or Article I, Section 8, of the Texas Constitution, or Chapter 73.[88]

On appeal, the plaintiffs tried to argue against Kaufman having a right to make use of this statute, despite the fact that it specifies electronic media as being covered. Rather, plaintiffs argued, Kaufman's reporting was not protected and he was not a media defendant because he "merely posts to the Internet."[89] The Court rejected the argument as erroneous on its face, and deemed Kauffman a media defendant (being that he was a regular blogger.) The court then dismissed the case against Kaufman outright because the plaintiffs failed to show how the article was **of**

---

86 Namely, Islamic Society of Arlington, Texas; Islamic Center of Irving; DFW Islamic Educational Center, Inc.; Dar Elsalam Islamic Center; Al Hedaya Islamic Center; and Islamic Association of Tarrant County.

87 Tex. Civ. Prac. & Rem. Code Ann. § 51.014(a)(6). This citation refers to a specific chapter of the Texas Civil Practices and Remedies Code.

88 291 S.W.3d at 138 (Tex. Ct. App. 2009).

89 Id.

or concerning them.[90] That is, since Kauffman didn't mention the plaintiffs in his article but rather named ICNA and IANT, who were not party to the suit, the plaintiffs could not fulfill their burden to show that the statement was about them. While the unique intersection between freedom of speech and the Internet will be more fully dealt with in Chapter Ten, Kaufman's case illustrates, amongst other things, the importance of knowing who is considered part of "the press," as members of the press may often take advantage of Federal and State statutes geared towards protecting their free speech rights.

For whatever reason, the plaintiffs in Kaufman's case were apparently unaware that the trend in United States jurisprudence is to construe "the press" broadly. As the Supreme Court stated over 70 years ago:

> The liberty of the press is not confined to newspapers and periodicals. It necessarily embraces pamphlets and leaflets. These indeed have been historic weapons in the defense of liberty, as the pamphlets of Thomas Paine and others in our own history abundantly attest. The press in its historic connotation comprehends every sort of publication which affords a vehicle of information and opinion.[91]

Indeed, the U.S. Supreme Court has suggested that, "By affording a privilege to some organs of communication but not to others, courts would inevitably be discriminating on the basis of content."[92] As the Internet continues to facilitate an exponential increase in public dialogue on matters of public concern, journalists who report using this medium should make every effort

---

90 The Texas Supreme Court declined to hear an appeal brought by the plaintiffs on January 15, 2010.

91 Lovell v. City of Griffin, 303 U.S. 444, 452 (1938). Emphasis added

92 Branzburg v. Hayes, 408 U.S. 665, 705 n.40 (1972).

to become knowledgeable regarding special protections for the press and when they apply. Regardless, if one has a question regarding media status, consultation with a duly licensed attorney familiar with the laws of that jurisdiction is essential.

3

STATEMENTS THAT CAN BE DEFAMATORY

“ The legitimate state interest underlying the law of libel is the compensation of individuals for the harm inflicted on them by defamatory falsehood."

> JUSTICE LEWIS F. POWELL, JR.,
> GERTZ V. ROBERT WELCH, INC.[93]

Despite the protections afforded free speech in the United States, the tort[94] of defamation exists to serve a valid purpose of compensation when one's reputation has been unjustifiably harmed.

Any statement that can be proven false, factual, concerning the plaintiff, published and harmful can form the basis of recovery by a plaintiff provided the plaintiff can show fault and/or damages when required by law.

---

93 Gertz v. Robert Welch, Inc., 418 U.S. 323, 341 (1974).

94 A tort is a civil wrong for which the one wronged may obtain (monetary) damages from a court ruling.

In addition, it is useful to note the following types of statements which *can* be considered defamatory at law. The below is in no way an exhaustive list.

❶ FALSE STATEMENTS OF FACT MADE WITHIN AN ORGANIZATIONAL OR WORKPLACE SETTING, INCLUDING BETWEEN COLLEAGUES, MAY BE DEFAMATORY

As stated in Chapter One, in order for a statement to be judged defamatory, it must be published (communicated to a **third party.**) There exists variance amongst states as to whether communication between members of an organization is considered published, so whether this kind of statement can form the basis of an actionable claim for defamation varies from jurisdiction to jurisdiction. A New Jersey court held that a campus security report, sent by security guards to the Director of Campus Safety and the Provost of Fairleigh Dickinson University, *was* 'published'[95] while a Missouri court held that a communication between two employees of different branches of a bank was *not*,[96] even though both cases involved communications that took place within a given organization. You never really know in advance whether the court will consider the communication published so err on the side of caution, even if you are speaking with a colleague, and generally avoid making defamatory statements, particularly in writing.

---

95 Jerolamon v. Farleigh Dickinson Univ., 488 A.2d 1064, 1067 (N.J. App. Div. 1985).

96 Perez v. Boatmen's Nat'l Bank, 788 S.W.2d 296, 300 (Mo. App. 1990). The Missouri Supreme Court had earlier held that "communications between officers of the same corporation in the due and regular course of the corporate business, or between different offices of the same corporation, are not publications to third persons." Hellisen v. Knaus Truck Lines, Inc., 370 S.W.2d 341, 344 (1963).

❷ FALSE STATEMENTS OF FACT MADE IN REFERENCE TO A SMALL IDENTIFIABLE GROUP MAY BE DEFAMATORY IF THE STATEMENT REFERS TO *ALL* MEMBERS OF THE GROUP.

In a case that appears in law school textbooks everywhere, several authors published a book that falsely depicted the models and saleswomen of a Neiman-Marcus store in Dallas as prostitutes, and salesmen as homosexuals.[97] Along with the corporation, three groups of Neiman-Marcus employees sued for defamation: all nine models, 15 of 25 salesmen, and 30 out of 382 saleswomen. The Court held that the models and salesmen had a right to sue, but that the saleswomen could not recover, on the basis that that the libelous statement only referred to a general class of people that was not small enough where it would affect each individual of the class. In other words, the Court found that being one of a small group of 25 meant that a given person could be identified, but that being one of 382 was unlikely to mean that every one of those 382 could be identified from the general statement.

As explained in Chapter Nine, the distinction between a small identifiable group and a larger more general class of people, though tenuous, is extremely significant. In light of a *lawfare* threat, never forget that while criticizing religion in general can never be defamatory (the U.S. does not have blasphemy laws), if one were to falsely refer to the members of a small church, mosque, or synagogue as a criminal group, even without naming the individual members, they could conceivably recover damages, if indeed the group is deemed small enough.

---

97 Neiman-Marcus v. Lait, 13 F.R.D. 311 (S.D.N.Y. 1952). This case was heard by the federal court for the Southern District of New York, and was reported in the Federal Rules Decisions.

❸ STATEMENTS OF FACT-BASED OPINION CAN BE THE
BASIS OF A DEFAMATION SUIT

Generally speaking, a statement of "pure" opinion may not serve as grounds for a defamation suit, since opinions are not factually true or false. When an opinion appears to be based on factual information, however, it may be actionable. As the Supreme Court explained, "Simply couching such statements in terms of opinion does not dispel these implications; and the statement, "In my opinion Jones is a liar," can cause as much damage to reputation as the statement, "Jones is a liar.""[98] The practical lesson derived from this is to not rely on constructions like "in my opinion" when discussing controversial issues, but to ensure that any underlying facts can be corroborated. For example, rather than saying "Nina is a liar" and hoping that it will be protected as opinion, stating instead "Nina is a liar BECAUSE..." supported by relevant facts or valid examples is the better route. Remember, if a statement can be proven false, it will not receive protection as opinion. The statements "Shirelle is ugly" or "Jackson is a poor public speaker" or "Norman is radical", on the other hand, are all of pure opinion.

❹ STATEMENTS THAT REFER TO SOMEONE INDIRECTLY
CAN BE DEFAMATORY

As stated previously, for a plaintiff to bring a defamation lawsuit, it must be based on a statement that is "of or concerning" him or her. Referring to someone does not have to be done by expressly naming them, but may be accomplished through implication, even fictionalization. For example, a California court held that, when a novel thinly veiled the identity of a psychiatrist

---

98 Milkovich v. Lorain Journal Co., 497 U.S. 1, 19 (1990).

and portrayed him in a defamatory fashion, the evidence was sufficient for the plaintiff psychiatrist to win his libel suit against the author and publisher.[99] Generally, the reference does not need to be by name, so long as a reasonable reader would believe that the statement refers to the plaintiff.[100]

❺ YOU MAY BE HELD LIABLE FOR REPUBLISHING A DEFAMATORY STATEMENT, AS WELL AS IF SOMEONE ELSE REPUBLISHES YOUR DEFAMATORY STATEMENT.

Let's say that Newspaper A publishes an article containing defamatory statements, and the same article is then reprinted by Newspaper B. *Both* newspapers A and B can be found liable for publishing the same article. While Newspaper B will be held liable as if it was the original publisher, Newspaper A can be held liable for its own publication as well as for the publication of Newspaper B. As the Virginia Supreme Court explained, "[i]t is well settled that the author or originator of a defamation is liable for a republication or repetition thereof by third persons, provided it is the natural and probable consequence of his act, or he has presumptively or actually authorized or directed its republication."[101]

NOTE: This rule generally does not apply to *Internet* republications, for reasons that will be addressed in Chapter Ten.

---

99 Bindrim v. Mitchell, 92 Cal.App.3d 61 (2d Dis. 1979). Note: the citation in this case is to the California court of appeal for the second district.

100 Peagler v. Phoenix Newspapers, Inc., 114 Ariz. 309, 315 (1977).

101 Weaver v. Beneficial Financial Co., 199 Va. 196, 199 (1957).

❻ ALTERING A QUOTE IN AND OF ITSELF, DOES NOT ALONE PROVIDE GROUNDS FOR DEFAMATION

Generally, placing a person's statement within quotation marks signifies a verbatim repetition. But what happens when a quoted statement is altered? In the case *Masson v. New Yorker Magazine*,[102] the Supreme Court held that even "a deliberate alteration of the words uttered by a plaintiff does not equate with knowledge of falsity"[103] demanded by the First Amendment under the *New York Times v. Sullivan* doctrine. Instead, the Court found that the altered 'quotations' needed only to be "substantially true," and sent the case down so that the trial court could consider whether there had been actual malice in altering the quotations. The Court explained that fabricated quotations could be libelous in one of two ways, "the quotation might injure because it attributes an untrue factual assertion to the speaker." Or, "the attribution may result in injury to reputation because the manner of expression or even the fact that the statement was made indicates a negative personal trait or an attitude the speaker does not hold."[104] In either case, the fact that the quote has been altered is not in and of itself determinative for purposes of a libel case. In sum, do not alter quotes unless absolutely necessary. Even though alteration does not itself give rise to a libel suit, if it results in injury to the original speaker in one of the two ways listed above, publishing such a statement may prove grounds for a claim of libel.

---

102 Masson v. New Yorker Mag., Inc., 501 U.S. 496 (1991).
103 Id. at 517.
104 Id. at 511

4

STATEMENTS THAT CANNOT BE DEFAMATORY

“ Is the making of a statement in the presence of two or more persons in any language, which incites, let us say, 'hostility' towards a group by reason of religion or race, capable of being made into a misdemeanor?”

THE NEW JERSEY SUPREME COURT,
STATE V. KLAPPROTT [105]

F or the same reasons that U.S. courts have established a series of constitutional protections aimed at ensuring freedom of speech and of the press, so too has American case law outlined several types of statements that may not be used as the basis for a defamation suit. As will be shown in this chapter, these include statements made directly to a plaintiff, statements of "pure opinion," statements that refer to the dead, and even reprehensibly racist speech.

---

[105] State v. Klapprott, 127 N.J.L. 395, 402 (1941). Note: N.J.L. refers to the New Jersey Lawyer reporter.

❶ STATEMENTS MADE DIRECTLY TO THE PLAINTIFF, AND NOT COMMUNICATED TO A THIRD PARTY

An essential component of a defamation claim is that the statement was communicated, either verbally or in writing, to a third party, i.e., the statement was "published." Traditionally, this question has come up in slander cases where someone made a defamatory comment directly to the plaintiff, but was overheard by another party. In those cases, courts often issued rulings dependent on whether third parties not only overheard the defamatory statement, but also understood it.[106] For example, if while speaking to Boris over the telephone, Alex makes a defamatory statement about Boris but only Boris hears the statement, it is not actionable. If Alex and Boris are at a party with mutual friends, however, and Alex speaks the defamatory statement about Boris so loudly that it is overheard by several people who know Boris at the party, the statement may be actionable. Note also, that if one writes a defamatory statement about a plaintiff in one's own notepad, and keeps the paper in a private desk drawer that is locked, then it is neither published nor communicated to the plaintiff and therefore, is not actionable. If you show your notes to a third party however, the statement may serve as a basis for a defamation lawsuit. But if your house were robbed, and the notes stolen from their private resting place, you would not be treated as having published the statement at law.

This same principle applies to letters sent directly to another, with one significant caveat. Hypothetically, if one were to send a sealed letter to person A that contained a defamatory statement about person A, it would not be considered "published,"

---

106 See, e.g., Economopoulos v. A.G. Pollard Co., 218 Mass. 294 (1914).

even if person A then shared it with others.[107] There is a notable exception, however, when "there is evidence to show that the party who sent it knew that some other person was in the habit of opening letters, or that in the ordinary course of business the contents of the letter would come to the knowledge of some third person."[108]

❷ STATEMENTS OF PURE OPINION

The previous chapter explained that opinions based on fact may be defamatory, but statements of "pure opinion" are not and can never form the basis of a defamation suit. Generally speaking, the court will look to whether or not a reasonable listener would have believed the statement to be a **factual assertion**. In a 1991 case from Arizona, a member of the state House of Representatives referred to a colleague, rhetorically asking, "What kind of communist do we have up there that thinks it's improper to protect your interests?"[109] When the case reached the Arizona state Supreme Court, it ruled that, while calling someone a communist was objectionable, the question as to whether it was a factual assertion had to be made by a jury.[110]

To illustrate, if Alex publishes the statement "Brett is an extremist" a jury may likely find that a reasonable listener may take this comment as one of opinion since whether or not someone is an extremist or radical is relatively unverifiable and not provable as false. Moreover, courts will afford protection for statements that cannot be interpreted as stating actual facts, which are "imaginative expression" or "rhetorical hyperbole."[111] The test is basically

---

107 Lyle v. Waddle, 144 Tex. 90 (1945).
108 Roberts v. English Mfg. Co., 155 Ala. 414, 416 (1904).
109 Yetman v. English, 168 Ariz. 71, 73 (1991).
110 Id at 77.
111 Letter Carriers v Austin, 418 U.S. 264 (1974) at 53-55

whether a reasonable person will imply a factual truth to the matter asserted and if indeed this is the case [*i.e.,* whether the factual statement asserted is verifiable.] For instance, the statement "Renee is a contemptible human being" would not be actionable because Renee's contemptibility, *vel non,* "is not the kind of empirical question a fact-finder can resolve."[112]

NOTE: Whether a statement is one of fact or opinion may be a question for either the court or the jury, depending on what state the action is brought in.

❸ STATEMENTS PURPORTEDLY "DEFAMING" THE DEAD

Defamation is an actionable claim; that is, it may form the basis of a lawsuit because of the damage it does to one's reputation. It is a personal claim that cannot be brought by another. Therefore, once a person dies, no defamation claim may be brought on behalf of the deceased. As the Supreme Court of Missouri put it nearly a century ago, "In libel every tub stands on its own bottom."[113] However, when a statement referencing a deceased has implications for someone living, for instance via allegations that actions by a deceased person resulted in his living child being a bastard, the living person may bring suit. However, the claim may only be brought *on behalf of the living child, never on behalf of the deceased.* The mere fact that someone is related to a deceased individual allegedly defamed does not, in and of itself, bestow standing to litigate on behalf of the dead. As the Massachusetts Supreme Court explained:

> The general rule is that a libel upon the memory of a deceased person that does not directly cast any personal re-

---

112 Yetman v. English, 168 Ariz. 71, 73 (1991), at 81
113 Diener v. Star-Chronicle Publ'g Co., 230 Mo. 613, 625 (1910).

flection upon his relatives does not give them any right of action, although they may have thereby suffered mental anguish or sustained an impairment of their social standing among a considerable class of respectable people of the community in which they live by the disclosure that they were related to the deceased.[114]

This a very important distinction for journalists writing about religion or terrorism, since other nations may indeed allow judicial or quasi-judicial actions on behalf of dead persons, as a Canadian case brought by one Syed Soharwardy demonstrates all too well.

Two Canadian media sources republished cartoons from Denmark that depicted the Muslim prophet Mohammed. In response, Syed Soharwardy of the Islamic Supreme Council of Canada and the Edmonton Council of Muslim Communities brought complaints[115] before the Alberta Human Rights and Citizenship Commission against the two media organizations, the *Western Standard* and the *Jewish Free Press*, along with their publishers, Ezra Levant and Richard Bronstein, respectively. Soharwardy alleged that the republication of the cartoons personally defamed him due to his status as a descendant of Mohammed and that the cartoons further linked him and his family to terrorism. Bronstein and the Jewish Free Press settled with Soharwardy, but Levant resisted,[116] leading Soharwardy to eventually withdraw his complaint.[117] Despite Soharwardy's withdrawal, the Alberta Human Rights and Citizenship Commission refused to dismiss the case for another six months, at

---

114 Hughes v. New England Newspaper Publ'g Co., 312 Mass. 178, 179 (1942).

115 http://ezralevant.com/Soharwardy_complaint.pdf

116 http://ezralevant.com/Response_to_complaint.pdf

117 Graeme Morton, Muslim Leader Drops Ezra Levant Cartoon Complaint, Nat'l Post (Feb. 11, 2008), http://www.nationalpost.com/news/canada/story.html?id=303895

which point it finally did[118] with an 11-page ruling that was critical of Levant. Levant responded by expressing frustration "Because I haven't been given my freedom of the press. I've simply had the government censor approve what I said. That's a completely different thing."[119]

❹ GROUP LIBEL

In marked contrast to the European "hate speech" laws that will be addressed in Chapter Nine, the United States has rejected the concept of **group libel**. The question quoted at the beginning of this chapter was answered by the New Jersey Supreme Court in the negative, finding unconstitutional a New Jersey statute that criminalized:

> Any person who shall, in the presence of two or more persons, in any language, make or utter any speech, statement or declaration, which in any way incites, counsels, promotes, or advocates hatred, abuse, violence or hostility against any group or groups of persons residing or being in this state by reason of race, color, religion or manner of worship[120]

Similarly, a New York court dismissed a charge of criminal libel resulting from publications that allegedly libeled "All persons of the Jewish Religion."[121] In an opinion that cited a number of contemporaneous cases, the Court said of the publications at issue:

> They are palpably the outpourings of a fanatical and bigoted mind.... And when one realizes how many forms of

---

118 http://ezralevant.com/Complaint%20rejected.pdf
119 http://ezralevant.com/2008/08/punished-first-acquitted-later.html
120 N.J.Rel.Stat. §2:157B-5, cited in State v. Klapprott, 127 N.J.L. 395, 396 (1941).
121 People v. Edmonson, 168 Misc. 142 (1938).

religion might consider themselves libeled and seek legal redress, were our laws so extended, and when we reflect on how our courts might, in such event, find themselves forced into the position of arbiters of religious truth, it is apparent that more would be lost than could be gained by attempting to protect the good name of a religion by an appeal to the criminal law.[122]

In much the same vein, when asked shortly after World War II to consider whether the United States should adopt the concept, *"the Commission on the Freedom of the Press was unanimously opposed to the enactment of group libel legislation."*[123] [Italics in the original.] Similarly, after the city of St. Paul, Minnesota passed an ordinance that criminalized actions or the display of symbols that aroused "anger, alarm or resentment in others on the basis of race, color, creed, religion or gender,"[124] the United State Supreme Court ruled it unconstitutional. The case centered around a plaintiff that engaged in cross burning and was subsequently charged under the statute just mentioned. The court ruled the law "facially unconstitutional, because it imposes special prohibitions on those speakers who express views on the disfavored subjects of 'race, color, creed, religion or gender.'"[125] The city's "desire to communicate to minority groups that it does not condone the 'group hatred' of bias-motivated speech does not justify selectively silencing speech on the basis of its content."[126] The court reiterated that the First Amendment generally prohibits government from outlawing speech or conduct because of

---

122 Id. at 154.

123 Zechariah Chafee, Jr., *Government and Mass Communications, Vol. I: A Report from the Commission on Freedom of the Press*, The University of Chicago Press, Chicago, Ill. 1947.

124 St. Paul, Minn., Legis. Code § 292.02 (1990).

125 R.A.V. v. City of St Paul, 505 U.S. 381 (1992).

126 Supreme Court Syllabus for R.A..V v. City of St Paul, 505 U.S. 378 (1992).

"disapproval of the ideas expressed." Though the constitution has been interpreted by the Supreme Court to permit speech regulation in a few limited areas, because of their constitutionally proscribable content (ex. obscenity, defamation, and incitement to immediate unlawful violence), it may not make "content discrimination." Hence, while the government may punish libel, "it may not make the further content discrimination of proscribing only libel critical of the government,"[127] for example. The government may not regulate speech "based on hostility—or favoritism—towards the underlying message expressed,"[128] and should not be able to "drive certain ideas or viewpoints from the marketplace."[129] Because the First Amendment does not permit the Government "to impose special prohibitions on those speakers who express views on disfavored subjects,"[130] one is indeed free to be a bigot in this country and express notions of racial supremacy, you are generally allowed to burn a cross and display a Nazi swastika, as long as you are not violating an ordinance that is not speech-related (*i.e.,* public nuisance, vandalism, or public endangerment laws). As the Court concluded, "Let there be no mistake about our belief that burning a cross in someone's front yard is reprehensible. But St. Paul has sufficient means at its disposal to prevent such behavior without adding the First Amendment to the fire."[131]

Therefore, so long as one is writing within the United States, a group may only recover for defamation if it meets the

---

127 R.A.V. v. City of St. Paul, 505 U.S. 377, 384 (1992).

128 Id. At 386.

129 Id. At 387 [citing Simon & Schuster, Inc. v. Members of the N.Y. State Crime Victims Bd., 502 U.S. 105, 116 (1991)].

130 Id. At 391.

131 Id. at 396.

standards set in the *Neiman-Marcus* case[132] cited in the preceding chapter. You *cannot* win a lawsuit in the United States for blasphemy or defamation of religion. A cornerstone of American liberal democracy is the right to question and criticize the government, the right to be critical of religion, and of course, the related concept of separation between church (or mosque or synagogue) and state. The United States does not have "hate speech" laws outlawing communications offensive to members of any religious faith, and for good reason.

---

132 Neiman-Marcus v. Lait, 13 F.R.D. 311 (S.D.N.Y. 1952).

5

DEFENSES AGAINST A DEFAMATION CLAIM

" This Word 'false' must have some Meaning, or else how came it there? ... No, the Falshood [sic] makes the Scandal, and both make the Libel"

ANDREW HAMILTON, STATED IN DEFENSE
OF HIS CLIENT JOHN PETER ZENGER [133]

There are three basic defenses to defamation claims, of which **the truth** is by far the strongest. If a plaintiff cannot prove that an allegedly defamatory statement is false, under U.S. law, *the plaintiff cannot recover*. Second, statements of **opinion** are generally not defamatory. Finally, there are certain **privileges** afforded defendants. That is, instances in which statements that could otherwise be defamatory are given special protection, such as statements given during a court proceeding. A number of states have legislated an additional

---

133 This famous case, which took place during the colonial period, established truth as a defense for claims of libel. A Brief Narrative of the Case and Tryal of John Peter Zenger, Printer of the New-York Weekly Journal (1736), available at
http://www.nycourts.gov/history/elecbook/zenger_tryal/pg15.htm.

defense to predatory lawsuits designed specifically to suppress speech. The laws are known as anti-SLAPP statutes (the acronym derived from "strategic litigation against public participation"). Anti-SLAPP statutes will be addressed in Chapter Six.

❶ THE TRUTH

During the Colonial period, the typesetter of a small newspaper was "charged with Printing and publishing *a certain false, malicious, seditious and scandalous Libel.*"[134] His attorney, Andrew Hamilton, stated in his defense that if a statement were true, it could not be libelous. Despite the admonitions of the judge in the case, the jury decided that truth was a bar to a defamation claim. This was a watershed moment in the American development of defamation laws—solidifying the concept that truth is an absolute defense. As previous chapters have illustrated, this does not mean that an entire statement must be perfectly accurate, rather the statement must be "substantially true." That is, if charged with libel, a defendant is not required to validate every single word used. Rather, she must only show that the "the substance, the gist, the sting, of the matter is true."[135] So, even if a defendant says horrible things about a plaintiff, no matter how bad, if the substance of the statements are factually true, the plaintiff cannot recover in a court of law.

❷ OPINION

Statements of opinion are not protected unless they are of "pure opinion." Accordingly, stating that an individual is "a terrible person," though objectionable, would not give rise to a claim for defamation, unless it were accompanied by at least an implication

---

134 Id.

135 Gomba v. McLaughlin, 180 Colo. 232, 236 (1972)

of underlying facts that led to the opinion, since one's opinion is, objectively speaking, neither true nor false but a personal viewpoint.

When stated opinions imply a factual basis, the defense gets more complicated. For example, as the Massachusetts Supreme Court held, "If a statement of critical opinion is based on assumed, non-defamatory facts, the First Amendment forbids the law of libel from redressing the injury."[136] In that case, the plaintiff was a sportscaster lambasted by a sports magazine as the worst in the area. Further, the magazine bitingly remarked that he was "The only newscaster in town who is enrolled in a course for remedial speaking."[137] In truth, the newscaster was not enrolled in any such course; the magazine was being sarcastic to make a point. The Court ruled that, in context, the statement could reasonably be taken to mean that the sportscaster *should* have been enrolled in such a course and dismissed the case.

Generally, in determining whether a statement is "pure opinion" or not, the Court will look to four factors:

* The specific language used
* Whether the statement is verifiable
* The general context in which the statement was made, and
* The broader context in which the statement appeared

How would these factors be applied? In the Massachusetts case mentioned above, the Court looked at the specific statements made, namely that the plaintiff was the "worst" sportscaster and that he "was enrolled" in a remedial-speaking course. Next, the

---

136 Myers v. Boston Mag. Co., 380 Mass. 336, 345 (1980).
137 Id at 338.

Court looked at each statement to see if it could be verified. The first, calling the plaintiff "the worst" could not be verified, but the second seemed to be verifiable, depending on whether the sportscaster was, in fact, enrolled in such a course. That meant that the Court had to consider the statement's context. When it did, the Court found that the statement's context "partake(s) of an ancient, lively tradition of criticizing, even lampooning, performers."[138] Hence, the court ruled this was a form of satire. Similarly, when the popular cartoon series *South Park* attempted to satirize Islam's prophet Muhammad by depicting him as a cartoon and positing that he had a supernatural ability to remain free of criticism, no lawsuits could be brought against the cartoon's creators in the United States on that factual basis.[139] Unfortunately, Comedy Central chose to heavily censor the two-episode arc after receiving threats of violence, evidencing a worrisome form of self-censorship that will be discussed more fully in Chapter Seven.

Still, as cautioned in previous chapters, it is generally more prudent to clearly separate one's opinions from facts that may appear to underlie them or to make sure that one is able to verify those facts.

❸ PRIVILEGES

While the defenses of truth and opinion represent absolute protections against defamation lawsuits, there is an additional category of defenses called **privileges**. When a defendant can

---

138 Id at 344.

139 However, self-described descendants of the Islamic prophet Muhammad have brought legal complaints of libel or "hate speech" in Europe and Canada. Recently, the Danish newspaper Politiken apologized for reprinting Muhammad cartoons in 2008, after a Saudi attorney threatened a lawsuit on behalf of eight organizations and allegedly, 94,923 descendants of Muhammad. See Patrick Goodenough, 'Descendants of Mohammed' Confront Newspapers Over Cartoons, Demanding Apologies and Eyeing Lawsuits, CNS News (Mar. 2, 2010), http://www.cnsnews.com/news/article/62122.

establish that he or she had a privilege to make a defamatory statement, even if the plaintiff can prove every element of the claim, the defendant will prevail.

There are three types of privileges: **absolute, qualified**, and **conditional**.

ABSOLUTE PRIVILEGES: For this category of privilege the defendant's intent doesn't matter at all, even if motivated by malice. A plaintiff can invoke an absolute privilege when his/her statement was made:

> During and as part of a judicial proceeding. The privilege here extends to all statements made during legal proceedings, whether by the judge, attorneys, parties or witnesses. The statement need not be made inside the courtroom, as long as the speech is relevant to the proceeding. This includes witness testimony and statements made to or by a lawyer during a deposition. Remember: It is never permissible to give false testimony in a court proceeding. Recovering for defamation and the crime of perjury are separate and distinct issues. One should never lie in a judicial proceeding lest s/he be charged with perjury.

> OR

> During Legislative proceedings (federal, state, or local.) This rule extends to town boards and other formal hearings. The privilege also applies to legislators acting in a legislative function, to witnesses called during legislative proceedings, and may apply to statements made during administrative proceedings, depending on the jurisdiction.[140]

---

140 For example, the Wisconsin Supreme Court held that statements made to a city council during a public meeting merited only a conditional privilege in Vultaggio v. Yasko, 572 N.W.2d 450 (Wis. 1998).

Hence, a plaintiff can not recover for a statement made during either judicial or legislative proceedings.

Moreover:

* *All* **federal officials** have an absolute privilege but only for statements made in the course of their official conduct.[141]

* **High-level state officials** generally have the same privilege, though lower-level state and local officials generally do not. The limits of this privilege vary from state to state.

* If a plaintiff **consents** to the publication of a statement, the statement is absolutely privileged.

* Any communication between **spouses** is absolutely privileged. This is known as the "marital privilege," "spousal privilege" or "husband-wife privilege."[142]

CONDITIONAL/QUALIFIED PRIVILEGES: Unlike the above privileges, the following are privileges that can be lost depending on the defendant's intent behind making the statement. In such cases, when a defendant claims a privilege, the plaintiff may introduce evidence proving the defendant abused the privilege, such as by demonstrating actual malice. Malice, in this regard, is defined as nefarious intent, dislike, or intent to injure.

---

141 Barr v. Matteo, 360 U.S. 564 (1959).
142 "The basis of the immunity given to communications between husband and wife is the protection of marital confidences, regarded as so essential to the preservation of the marriage relationship as to outweigh the disadvantages to the administration of justice which the privilege entails." Wolfle v. U.S. 291 U.S. 7, 14 (1934).

* **Reporting on public proceedings** does not carry the same absolute protection as participating in public proceedings, but carries with it a conditional privilege at common law. In these cases, a court will look to how accurately and fairly the statement reports on the proceeding (as explained previously in Chapter One).

* **Neutral reportage.** This is a conditional privilege only recognized by some jurisdictions. While repeating a defamatory statement could expose a person to liability, several courts have recognized the need to protect a member of the news media who needs to repeat potentially defamatory statements in the context of a story, so long as the report is accurate and neutral. As the Second Circuit Court of Appeals held, "when a responsible, prominent organization ... makes serious charges against a public figure, the First Amendment protects the accurate and disinterested reporting of those charges, regardless of the reporter's private views regarding their validity."[143] So, when the *New York Times* reported that the National Audubon Society had called a group of scientists "paid liars," the Court held it essential that "the press be afforded the freedom to report such charges without assuming responsibility for them."[144]

* Generally, if the speaker and recipient share a **common interest**, it may qualify for conditional protection. This could include members of private organizations speaking to one another. Courts are reluctant to extend this privilege, however, and it should not be relied upon.

* **A defendant has the right to protect his/her own interests.** If one's interest in the issue is considered sufficiently important, such as reporting stolen property or informing the police of a suspect, then this conditional privilege may apply, but it is limited. For example, say-

143 Edwards v. Nat'l Audubon Soc'y, 556 F.2d 113, 120 (2d Cir. 1977).
144 Id.

ing to the police "I think it was Robert who stole my car" when being questioned might well be protected, but falsely adding "and he cheats on his taxes" would probably not be protected, as it is irrelevant to protecting one's interest in the matter at hand (i.e. the car theft.)

* **Statements made in the public interest.** Similarly, if someone can show that he or she is making a statement **in the public interest**, such as informing a public official, this privilege can apply.[145] (See the Anti-SLAPP chapter which follows.)

Free and open discussion on matters of public interest is the bedrock of the American Constitution, and as the Supreme Court has expressed, safeguarding the means of enlightening the public "is essential to the securing of an informed and educated public opinion with respect to a matter which is of public concern."[146] For this reason, a number of jurisdictions have begun enacting laws specifically aimed at preventing lawsuits that seek to prevent people from participation in the public interest, with a new type of statute known as an anti-SLAPP law.

---

145 Interestingly, the United Kingdom only recently granted full judicial recognition to such a privilege, in Jameel v. Wall St. J. Europe Sprl, [2006] UKHL 44 [Opinions by the House of Lords]. Available online at
http://www.publications.parliament.uk/pa/ld200506/ldjudgmt/jd061011/jamee.pdf
146 Thornhill v. Alabama, 310 U.S. 88, 104 (1940).

6

ANTI-SLAPP LAWS

❝ The freedom of speech and of the press guaranteed by the Constitution embraces at the least the liberty to discuss publicly and truthfully all matters of public concern, without previous restraint or fear of subsequent punishment.❞

JUSTICE FRANK MURPHY,
THORNHILL V. ALABAMA [147]

Strategic Lawsuits Against Public Participation (SLAPP) are predatory lawsuits, often defamation claims, that are brought in an attempt to prevent individuals or groups from speaking about matters of public concern or participating in governmental functioning. The goal is intimidation via the process of lawsuit, as opposed to recovering damages for wrongful harm done. As the Federal Anti-SLAPP Project website explains, "SLAPPs silence and punish those who engage in public

---

147 Id. at 101-02.

participation, chilling speech that is essential to the functioning of our democracy and to the public interest."[148]

These lawsuits can have an impact on both the freedom of speech and press clauses of the First Amendment, as well as the right "to petition the Government for a redress of grievances." In response, a number of states,[149] with California leading the way, have enacted statutes or created through judicial decisions, a countermeasure known as an "anti-SLAPP."

The utility and limitation of anti-SLAPP laws against Islamist lawfare is best illustrated by case examples, some of which appeared in an article[150] published by the *Riverside Press-Examiner* in conjunction with a conference on "Libel Lawfare" organized by the authors which took place on May 19, 2009 in Washington, DC.

In 2002, the Anti-Defamation League's regional director and regional board chairman wrote and published a letter to California's schools Superintendent urging investigation into whether state funding to the GateWay Academy charter school system was being unlawfully used to promote religion.

The letter called attention to the superintendent of the GateWay Academy, Khadija Ghafur, and "referred accurately to news reports stating that plaintiff (Ghafur) was an officer of 'Muslims of the Americas,' that Muslims of the Americas was a corporate front for Al-Fuqra, and that members of Al-Fuqra had

---

148 The Public Participation Project, www.anti-slapp.org (last visited Nov. 23, 2010).

149 A listing of these statutes is available on the Legal Project's website. Jacquelyn Kline, Anti-SLAPP Statutes in the US by State, The Legal Project (Jan. 14, 2009), http://www.legal-project.org/article/149.

150 Aaron Eitan Meyer, Squelching Free Speech: Don't Let 'Lawfare,' Legal Ploys Chill Public Debate on Radical Islam, The Press-Enterprise (June 6, 2009), http://www.pe.com/localnews/opinion/localviews/stories/PE_OpEd_Opinion_S_op_07_meyer_loc.4d0ace3.html.

committed murders and bombings in the United States."[151] Ghafur then filed suit in San Francisco against the league and its officers, claiming that the public letter constituted libel against her.

In 2007, Yale University Press published a book by counterterrorism expert Matthew Levitt of the Washington Institute for Near East Policy. Entitled *Hamas: Politics, Charity and Terrorism in the Service of Jihad,* the book alleged that several U.S.-based charities had funded the designated foreign terrorist organization, Hamas. Among the named organizations was Kids in Need of Development, Education and Relief Inc., better known as KinderUSA. KinderUSA sent a letter to Yale University Press demanding a retraction.

When the publisher refused, KinderUSA filed a libel lawsuit in Los Angeles Superior Court against Yale University Press, the Washington Institute, and Levitt.

All too many defendants in situations such as these have been forced to surrender, facing bankruptcy from legal fees long before their cases could be heard, and regardless of the merit of their writings. Both the Anti-Defamation League and Levitt, however, were able to make use of a legal innovation enacted by the California Legislature in 1993. Known as an anti-SLAPP statute, this law functions as a legal mechanism aimed at preventing and punishing lawsuits designed to hinder legitimate public dialogue. When the Anti-Defamation League made this motion, the trial court dismissed the lawsuit, a ruling that was upheld on appeal. The judge determined that the questions raised by the ADL were of sufficient importance to allow public discussion thereof without fear of predatory lawsuits.

---

151 Ghafur v. Bernstein, 131 Cal. App. 4th 1230, 1234 (Cal. Ct. App. 2005).

In the Yale University Press case, after the defendants filed the anti-SLAPP motion, KinderUSA mysteriously dropped the lawsuit altogether, saying only that it had "underestimated the costs involved."[152]

By contrast, recall the case against Joe Kaufman. The suit concerned an article by Kaufman published on September 28, 2007, at FrontPageMag.com. Entitled "Fanatic Muslim Family Day,"[153] the piece alerted readers to a then-forthcoming event, "Muslim Family Day," at the Six Flags Over Texas amusement park, hosted by the Islamic Circle of North America (ICNA) and the Islamic Association of North Texas (IANT). Kaufman called ICNA "a radical Muslim organization that has physical ties with the Muslim Brotherhood and financial ties to Hamas" and stated that, "ICNA has also been involved in the financing of Al-Qaeda." On October 14, 2007, Kaufman led a lawful and peaceful protest against ICNA outside the amusement park.

Seven Dallas-area Muslim groups responded by filing a libel lawsuit and restraining order against Kaufman—despite the fact that the article never mentioned any of them. As Kaufman testified, he had "no knowledge that the majority of the entities [that sued him] even existed."[154] Since Texas does not have an anti-SLAPP statute, Kaufman's case continued to drag on for over a year and a half, until the Texas Court of Appeals for the Second District dismissed the lawsuit on June 25, 2009. In dismissing the lawsuit on appeal, the Court agreed with Kaufman that:

---

152 According to Todd Gallinger, KinderUSA's attorney. See Judith Miller, Bullies Back Off: Libel Suits vs. Terror Foes Lose Steam, N.Y. Post (Oct. 10, 2007), http://www.nypost.com/p/news/opinion/opedcolumnists/bullies_back_off_aH29HnEWnVLu IUe4HRDtiJ.

153 Kaufman, supra note 84.

154 Kaufman v. Islamic Soc'y of Arlington, 291 S.W.3d 130, 137 (Tex. App. 2d Dist. 2009).

There is simply no indication to a reasonable reader of Kaufman's article that "those involved" meant the sponsors of the event other than ICNA or IANT, because the article did not inform the reader that there were any such other sponsors.[155]

Given the suit against Kaufman appeared frivolous on its face, it's unfortunate that he could not have availed himself of an anti-SLAPP statute enabling a judge to dismiss it shortly after it was filed, thereby saving both Kaufman and the court, time and money spent defending his rights.

Yet even when anti-SLAPP statutes are available, it is not always possible for defendants to make use of them effectively. In 2003, the Islamic Society of Boston (ISB) purchased a parcel of land in Roxbury, Massachusetts from the City of Boston's Redevelopment Authority with the goal of constructing a 70,000-square-foot mosque. Several news outlets and local Jewish groups protested the construction of the mosque, alleging that ISB had connections to terrorist organizations and that the City of Boston had sold the parcel below market value.

In response, ISB sued for libel and infringement of its civil rights, naming eight media and nine non-media individuals and groups as defendants, including the local Fox affiliate WFXT-TV and counterterrorism expert Steven Emerson. The non-media defendants moved to dismiss the suit on anti-SLAPP grounds. The trial court denied the motion, limiting the protection of Massachusetts' anti-SLAPP statute to activity that directly petitioned the government.[156] The website for Emerson's organization, The Investigative Project on Terrorism, reports that

---

155 Id.
156 Islamic Soc'y of Boston v. Boston Herald, Inc., 21 Mass. L. Rep. 441 (Sup. Ct. 2006).

the lawsuit was curiously dropped[157] by the plaintiff in 2007, soon after the discovery process began and two weeks before ISB's most vulnerable witnesses were to be deposed.[158]

Anti-SLAPP statutes differ from state to state, while there is a great need for uniformity. Note also the weakness of an anti-SLAPP statute lies in the fact that one must be sued in order to take advantage of it. In other words it can not, and does not, prevent a frivolous lawsuit from being filed in the first place. Rather, anti-SLAPP statutes tend to provide, as discussed, an expedited dismissal procedure, and often result in punitive damages as well as attorneys fees.

The Federal Anti-SLAPP Project has been lobbying for a federal statute[159] that would eliminate some of the difficulties presented by the fact that anti-SLAPP laws are neither uniform nor universal, but a word of caution remains. To make use of an anti-SLAPP motion, one must first be sued. Fear of such lawsuits, however, has led to a culture of self-censorship that has deeply chilled free and open discourse on Islam, radicalized Islam, terrorism, and terror financing, as the following chapter will illustrate.

Anti-SLAPP motions are especially important protections for journalists who are reporting on issues of terror financing. As Daniel Pipes put it,

---

157 The discovery process is a pre-trial phase in a lawsuit whereby each party is able to obtain evidence from the other relevant to the issue at trial. In the ISB case, the defendants would have presumably been able to discover ISB's financial statements in order to prove the truth of the matters they asserted.

158 A deposition, or examination before trial, is the taking of out of court testimony of a witness that is reduced to writing for later use in court. Islamic Society of Boston, et al. v. Boston Herald, et al., The Investigative Project on Terrorism, http://www.investigativeproject.org/case/367 (last visited Nov. 23, 2010).

159 This bill, the "Citizen Participation Act" was introduced in the House as H.R. 4364 by Rep. Steve Cohen, and is available online at http://www.anti-slapp.org/sites/default/files/COHEN_071_xml_0.pdf

It is time to enact a uniform, federal anti-SLAPP legislation, as is now being proposed under the name of the "The Citizen Participation in Government and Society Act." Among other benefits, this will protect researchers and activists dealing with radical Islam and terrorism from predatory use of the legal system.[160]

To this end, U.S. Representative Steve Cohen (D) introduced H.R. 4364 on December 16, 2009. Entitled the "Citizen Participation Act of 2009," the bill would establish uniform protection throughout the United States.[161]

---

160 Daniel Pipes, Waging Jihad by American Courts, American Spectator (Mar. 2010), available at http://www.danielpipes.org/8131/jihad-through-american-courts.

161 Referred to the House Subcommittee on Courts and Competition Policy on April 26, 2010, the bill may be viewed here: http://frwebgate.access.gpo.gov/cgi-bin/getdoc.cgi?dbname=111_cong_bills&docid=f:h4364ih.txt.pdf

7

SELF-CENSORSHIP

" Our touchstones are that acceptable limitations must neither affect 'the impartial distribution of news' and ideas, nor because of their history or impact constitute a special burden on the press, *nor deprive our free society of the stimulating benefit of varied ideas because their purveyors fear physical or economic retribution solely because of what they choose to think and publish.*"

[Emphasis Added]

JUSTICE JOHN MARSHALL HARLAN, II,
CURTIS PUBLISHING CO. v. BUTTS [162]

While libel lawsuits have resulted in articles being retracted and text being removed from websites, the *fear* of suit (and violence) is, in all likelihood, an even better tool for those who wish to silence public speech on militant Islam, terrorism and its sources of financing, before it gets published. The extent of self-censorship in this subject area is

---

162 Curtis Publ'g Co. v. Butts, 388 U.S. 130, 151 (1967) (internal citations omitted).

unknowable by its very nature, leaving the public at times unaware of the fact that information has been kept from widespread dissemination and public discussion.

It is possible to roughly delineate three major types of Islamist-influenced self-censorship, which will be considered in turn:

❶ Publishers declining to publish books and reneging on contracts for materials with a focus on Islam, its prophet Mohammad, terrorism and its sources of financing (collectively herein "IMTF");

❷ Members of the media failing to report on crucial issues related to IMTF; and

❸ Censoring or "modifying" articles, books, television programs, etc. that focus on IMTF or the satirization thereof.

Lawfare targeting free speech is often complemented by threats of physical violence, a combination that has worked all too effectively to achieve an unwarranted chilling effect on free speech.

❶ PUBLISHERS DECLINING TO PUBLISH BOOKS AND RENEGING ON CONTRACTS[163]

Attempts to suppress the free discussion of IMTF take many different forms, but the most difficult to document is self-censorship. Indeed, Islamist lawfare could be likened to an iceberg, with self-censorship representing the immense mass lurking

---

163 Much of the material contained in this chapter first appeared in Aaron Eitan Meyer, Islamist-Friendly Self-Censorship in the United States Marches On, Legal Project Blog (Aug. 14, 2009, 1:57 PM), http://www.legal-project.org/blog/2009/08/islamist-friendly-self-censorship-in-the-united.

beneath opaque waves, and its chilling effect extending farther than the eye can see.

On August 12, 2009, the *New York Times* reported[164] that Yale University Press' then-upcoming book on the Danish Muhammad cartoons, entitled *The Cartoons That Shook the World*, would not only fail to include the cartoons themselves, but would also be entirely devoid of any images depicting Muhammad. The *Times* article further reported that Yale had consulted "two dozen authorities, including diplomats and experts on Islam and counterterrorism" and that these unnamed individuals unanimously stated that the book should contain no images of Muhammad. The rationale for this recommendation was, according to special adviser to the secretary general of the United Nations Ibrahim Gambari, "you can count on violence if any illustration of the prophet is published."[165]

Yale Press' response is eerily reminiscent of when Random House attracted considerable attention in 2008 for pulling the novel *The Jewel of Medina* after it received predictions of outrage and violence resulting from its forthcoming publication.[166] And while the home of U.K.-based Gibson Square's publisher was firebombed after he announced that he would publish the book, Beaufort Books eventually published the novel in the United States, a work of historical fiction centering on Muhammad's child bride Aisha, with no resultant violence.[167] Nor are publishing

164 Patricia Cohen, Yale Press Bans Images of Muhammad in New Book, N.Y. Times (Aug. 12, 2009), http://www.nytimes.com/2009/08/13/books/13book.html.

165 Id.

166 Edith Honan, Random House Pulls Novel on Islam, Fears Violence, Reuters (Aug. 7, 2008), http://www.reuters.com/article/newsOne/idUSN0736008820080807.

167 Daily Mail Reporter, Prophet bride book that provoked fire-bomb attack on British publisher printed in the U.S., The Daily Mail (October 7, 2008) http://www.dailymail.co.uk/news/article-1070932/Prophet-bride-book-provoked-bomb-attack-British-publisher-printed-U-S.html

companies the only parties engaging in this type of self censorship: television channel Comedy Central censored[168] a *South Park* episode in 2006 that was, ironically, *about* censorship, superimposing a black bar with the word "censored" over a cartoon image of Muhammad,[169] and approximately 25 newspapers[170] refused to run two 2007 *Opus* comic strip Sunday installments that poked fun at militant Islam. One must ask, who benefits from this type of self-censorship? How can a free society face certain threats if it is not able to at least laugh about them?[171]

Still, the most alarming aspect of self-censorship is that its chilling effect goes well beyond public perception. There is simply no way to determine how many books have not been published, or how many reports have been censored to avoid an unwanted reaction—whether that reaction is the specter of violence or threats of frivolous legal action.

The *Jewel of Medina* incident was itself but another in a growing number of examples of self-censorship. In December 2006, publisher Palgrave MacMillan reneged on its plans to publish a new, progressive translation of the Quran entitled *Quran: A Reformist Translation*.[172] It did so after receiving an

---

168 Lisa de Moreas, Comedy Central Again Steals 'South Park' Thunder, Wash. Post (Apr. 14, 2006), http://www.washingtonpost.com/wp-dyn/content/article/2006/04/13/AR2006041302212.html.

169 South Park was again censored by Comedy Central over its April 2010 two-part story that revolved around Muhammad's supposed supernatural ability to remain free from criticism and ridicule. Not only was Muhammad blocked by a "Censored" bar, but an entire section of dialogue was bleeped out as well.

170 Noel Sheppard, Newspapers Refuse to Run 'Opus' Comics with Muslim Reference, NewsBuster (Aug. 26, 2007, 7:52 PM), http://newsbusters.org/blogs/noel-sheppard/2007/08/26/newspapers-refuse-run-opus-comics-muslim-reference.

171 As comedian Penn Gillette said in an interview with Las Vegas Weekly, "we haven't tackled Islam because we have families... and I think the worst thing you can say about a group in a free society is that you're afraid to talk about it—I can't think of anything more horrific." See "A uniquely Weekly ranking of the personalities who define Las Vegas," by Las Vegas Weekly Staff, June 24, 2010. http://www.lasvegasweekly.com/news/2010/jun/24/celebrity-issue/

172 Quran: A Reformist Translation (Edip Yksel et al. trans., Brainbow Press, 2d rev. ed. 2010)

anonymous review from "a very well-established professor," to which the book's editor Edip Yuksel responded that shelving the book for this reason "was akin to a medieval publishing house turning down Martin Luther's 95 Theses after consulting 'a very well-established' Catholic Bishop!" While Brainbow Press eventually published the work, few are aware of its existence, much less of the controversy that surrounded its non-publication by Palgrave MacMillan.[173]

Perhaps an even better example of the unknown extent of self-censorship's reach comes from the following incident. "Faith Fighter"[174] is an online video game featuring various religious figures in combat, including Islam's prophet Muhammad. The game attracted considerable attention and controversy, but was removed[175] from creator Molleindustria's website after the Organization of Islamic Cooperation[176] (OIC) issued an official statement protesting the game.

"Faith Fighter" has since been reposted to Molleindustria's website, and appears in both "Normal" and "Uncensored" playable modes, with a warning that the game depicts Muhammad. The disclaimer then states "[i]f you feel that such a depiction would be offensive, we ask that you play the censored version of

(2007), available at http://www.irshadmanji.com/PDFS/ReformistTranslation.pdf.

173 Strangely enough, the second printing of the book is currently ranked fifteenth on Amazon.com's Bestseller list of books on Islam ... for children. http://www.amazon.com/Quran-Reformist-Translation-Modern-English/dp/0979671507/ref=sr_1_1?ie=UTF8&s=books&qid=1297188726&sr=8-1

174 Faith Fighter, http://www.newgrounds.com/portal/view/421199 (last visited Nov. 24, 2010).

175 OIC Wags Its Finger and "Faith Fighter" Is Removed, MediaWatchWatch (Apr. 28, 2009), http://www.mediawatchwatch.org.uk/2009/04/28/oic-wags-its-finger-and-faith-fighter-is-removed/.

176 On June 28, 2011, the Organization of the Islamic Conference changed its name to the Organization of Islamic Cooperation. The acronym OIC, which remains unaltered, will be used throughout this book.. See http://www.dawn.com/2011/06/29/oic-changes-name.html

the game in which the character's face has been removed. Or better yet, don't play the game at all."[177]

The story does not end there. The American television channel G4 describes itself[178] as "the one destination on television that feeds your addiction for the latest must-have tech gadgets, web culture and video games." It was not surprising, therefore, when it ran a 45-second "Indie Games" spot about "Faith Fighter" during a commercial break of the premier episode of the show "Web Soup" on June 7, 2009.

The brief spot summarized the game and its controversial nature, and the announcer, Kevin Pereira, mentioned the playable characters by name, noting that one could play as God, Jesus, Buddha, Ganesha and Budai. Unfortunately, not only did the segment completely omit mentioning that it was OIC pressure which led to the game being taken down, but it glaringly ignored the fact that there are **six** playable characters, even as Muhammad's unidentified image appeared directly behind the presenter as he listed each other character by name.

Self-censorship takes many forms, whether by refusing to include images in a book or television program, reneging on a contract to publish a fiction novel, or simply omitting crucial facts when reporting. The first step toward effectively countering this phenomenon is to bring these incidents into the light of public dialogue—precisely what proponents of Islamism seek to prevent and what this book seeks to achieve.

---

177 http://www.molleindustria.org/faith-fighter (last visited Feb. 7, 2011).

178 About G4, G4tv, http://g4tv.com/g4/about/index.html (last visited Nov. 24, 2010).

In the run-up to the 2008 U.S. presidential election, Andrew Walden investigated and wrote articles about connections between U.S.-Syrian citizen Tony Rezko, a fundraiser for Barack Obama, and Iraqi-British billionaire Nadhmi Auchi who wired Rezko $3.5 million in 2007 while Rezko was facing federal criminal charges.[179] On June 4, 2008, Rezko was found guilty by a federal district court in Illinois on 16 charges of mail and wire fraud, including a failure to report the $3.5 million loan from Auchi.[180] In response to Walden's and other articles highlighting the controversy, Auchi retained the British legal firm Carter-Ruck, and threatened suit against the publishers.[181] While several newspapers promptly removed articles mentioning Auchi from their websites, Walden and the *Hawai'i Free Press* refused, and the article at issue, with one minor revision, remains up on the *Hawai'i Free Press'* website. As Walden stated in an August 2008 article, media investigations about Auchi stalled because "attorneys from London law firm Carter-Ruck have for several months been flooding American and British newspapers and websites with letters demanding removal of material they deem 'defamatory' to their client."[182] Whatever the precise nature of Rezko and Auchi's relationship, which is important public information, the fact that

179 Obama bagman is sent to jail after failing to declare $3.5m payment by British tycoon, The Times, February 1, 2008.
http://www.timesonline.co.uk/tol/news/world/us_and_americas/us_elections/article3284825.ece
180 Rezko begins serving time immediately, WLS-TC (Local ABC News affiliate) June 5, 2008. http://abclocal.go.com/wls/story?section=news/politics&id=6185320
181 Andrew Walden, Iraqi Billionaire Threatens Reporters Investigating Rezko, MensNewsDaily (Aug. 26, 2008), http://mensnewsdaily.com/2008/08/26/iraqi-billionaire-threatens-reporters-investigating-rezko-affair/
182 Id.

the story has been suppressed due to legal intimidation is extremely troubling.

❸ CENSORING OR "MODIFYING" ARTICLES, BOOKS, TELEVISION PROGRAMS, *ETC.*

Dutch parliamentarian Geert Wilders is without question a controversial, even polarizing figure. His outspoken views on Islam and his movie *Fitna*, a 17-minute film that consists of incendiary sermons by Islamist clerics, Quranic verses, and graphic video of terrorist atrocities, have resulted in death threats,[183] threats of extradition[184] to Jordan for "blaspheming Islam," politicized court cases targeting Wilders in the Netherlands for "hate speech," and British appeasement of Muslims who threatened violence should he be allowed to enter the United Kingdom.[185]

Whatever one feels about his political views, the fact remains that Wilders' film *Fitna* consists almost entirely of quotes from the Quran and frothing harangues by Islamist clerics preaching death to "infidels." The film itself does not incite to any such acts, however, but rather condemns them. As the Muslims Against Sharia blog already pointed out,[186] exposing bigotry does not logically equate the exposer to holding the views he exposes. Raising awareness about how the likes of Al Qaeda use the Quran

---

183 Anthony Browne, Death Threats Force Unconventional Dutch MP Underground, Sunday Times (Nov. 20, 2004), http://www.timesonline.co.uk/tol/news/world/article393161.ece.

184 Deutsche Presse-Agentur, Dutch Islam Critic Meets Foreign Minister on Charges in Jordan, Monsters and Critics (June 26, 200, 6:16 GMT), http://www.monstersandcritics.com/news/middleeast/news/printer_1413393.php.

185 Aaron Eitan Meyer, A Fateful Decision for the UK, Legal Project Blog (Feb. 11, 2009, 11:01 AM), http://www.legal-project.org/blog/2009/02/a-fateful-decision-for-the-uk.

186 Geert Wilders on CNN: 'Al Qaeda of the Netherlands,' Muslims Against Sharia Blog (Mar. 1, 2009, 10:38 PM), http://muslimsagainstsharia.blogspot.com/2009/03/geert-wilders-on-cnn-al-qaeda-of.html.

to justify atrocious actions is neither bigoted nor "hate speech," and comparing Wilders to Al Qaeda, which issued a fatwa[187] ordering his "slaughter," is completely insupportable. Still, it is Wilders who has been charged with "hate speech" while the radical Imams featured in the film exhort their followers to commit acts of terrorism with impunity.

After a long trial, Wilders was finally acquitted by the Dutch court in June 2011. According to Dutch News, "the court ruled that some of Wilders' statements were insulting, shocking and *on the edge of legal acceptability*, [sic] but that they were made in the broad context of a political and social debate on the multi-cultural society."[188] The politician's opponents have already declared that they will go to regional and international tribunals to seek other sanctions against him for "blasphemy"—thereby effectively ignoring the Dutch ruling. That, in turn, raises questions about Wilders' accusers: were they cynically manipulating the Dutch legal system in order to impose elements of Shariah law? Was this trial simply intended to silence Wilders for his offense against Islam?

In fact, there is no legitimate comparison to be made between producing a film illustrating how doctrinal Islam is used to justify murder and actually inciting hatred, yet Wilders is overwhelmingly (falsely) portrayed as equivalent to militant Islamists—violent Shariah-enforcing Muslim jihadis.[189] To the contrary, it is essential that hate preachers be exposed, and calling for the punishment of one who exposes such heinous acts is

---

187 Al Qaeda Fatwa Against MP Wilders, NIS News (Feb. 28, 2008),
http://www.nisnews.nl/public/280208_5.htm.

188 http://www.dutchnews.nl/news/archives/2011/06/wilders_not_guilty_on_all_char.php

189 For perhaps the most egregious example, see Christine Romans, "Al Qaeda of the Netherlands" on Capitol Hill, CNN (Transcript of television program) Feb. 26, 1009. http://edition.cnn.com/TRANSCRIPTS/0902/26/ltm.02.html

illogical and dangerous. Blurring the lines between controversial and even objectionable speech on the one hand and actual incitement to acts of violence on the other, is antithetical to the principles of freedom of expression.

There are a number of instances mentioned throughout this book that point to deliberate self-censorship through modification or omission by the media. In fact, a secondary effect of media self-censorship has already begun to appear in the form of media standards that accord preferential treatment to some groups over others. As the next chapter will demonstrate, Islamist pressure and coercion has already begun to lead to a wholesale rewriting of how media cover matters of public concern.

8

MEDIA STANDARDS

" It is most unfortunate that the trend towards religious polarization continues to grow on account of the increasingly scurrilous assaults against Islam.... A section of the western media is a major factor in the formation of the collective misrepresentation about Islam and Muslims."

EKMELEDDIN IHSANOGLU,
SECRETARY-GENERAL OF THE ORGANIZATION
OF ISLAMIC COOPERATION
[See Chapter Nine][190]

" A responsible press is an undoubtedly desirable goal, but press responsibility is not mandated by the Constitution, and, like many other virtues, it cannot be legislated."

CHIEF JUSTICE WARREN E. BURGER,
MIAMI HERALD PUBLISHING CO. V. TORNILLO[191]

---

190 Forward to Second OIC Observatory Annual Report on Islamophobia, 2009, at pp. 1-2.
http://www.oic-un.org/document_report/Islamophobia_rep_May_23_25_2009.pdf
191 Miami Herald Publ'g Co. v. Tornillo, 418 U.S. 241, 256 (1974).

The preceding chapter dealt with the pervasive atmosphere of self-censorship that has arisen in part due to Islamist lawfare pressure. In much the same vein, recent statements and resolutions from the Organization of Islamic Cooperation (OIC) have specifically targeted the media, demonstrating an intent to influence reporting in the West. While Western democratic ideals rest on the bedrock of a free, un-censored and un-coerced press, the same cannot be said of the standards advocated by the OIC. The divide may be illustrated by the two quotes above. OIC Secretary-General Ekmeleddin Ihsanoglu made the first in 2008, while the second comes from a US Supreme Court opinion by Chief Justice Warren Burger.

Throughout the course of this book, we have shown how Islamist lawfare operates within the Western judicial system. A second and emerging area ripe for manipulation is the interpreta-tion and rewriting of journalistic codes of ethics.

A much-criticized UN Human Rights Council resolution sponsored by Egypt and the United States, "[r]ecognizes the moral and social responsibilities of the media and the importance that the media's own elaboration of voluntary codes of professional ethical conduct can play in combating racism, racial discrimination, xenophobia and related intolerance"[192] The OIC[193] appears to be using these terms as a smokescreen for its "Islamophobia" and "defamation of religion" campaigns. OIC pressure and maneuvering at the UN has already resulted in the yearly passage of U.N. Human Rights Council and General

---

192 UN Human Rights Council Resolution proposed by the Egypt and the United States. A/HRC/12/L.14/Rev.1, adopted October 2, 2009

193 Egypt is a charter member of the OIC, and will serve as the organization's president from 2011-2014. Egypt and the OIC, Egypt St. Info. Service, http://www2.sis.gov.eg/En/Politics/Foreign/IntlOrganizations/OIC/040313050000000001.ht m (last visited Nov. 24, 2010).

Assembly resolutions since 1999 bearing the title "Defamation of Religions," and later "Combating Defamation of Religions."[194]

While a complete analysis of the "Islamophobia" allegation routinely used by the OIC to further its political agenda is beyond the scope of this work, the OIC has made the media a cornerstone of its suppression strategy, routinely accusing Western journalists of "deliberate stereotyping of religions, their adherents and sacred persons in the media."[195] The OIC has even equated independent media reporting with "programmes and agendas pursued by extremist organizations and groups."[196] The OIC routinely smears those who write and speak about terrorism committed by self-described Islamist groups, as "racist" or "Islamophobic," or accuses them of 'defaming' religion for exposing the facts on the ground.

In an array of misleading and disingenuous statements, the OIC's second Observatory Report on Islamophobia[197] makes the conclusory proclamation that "The scourge of Islamophobia prevalent in the Western mind and media is substantiated by the writings and Reports of well-known Western researchers and columnists."[198] Needless to say, the Report fails to substantiate any such "scourge."

194
http://unbisnet.un.org:8080/ipac20/ipac.jsp?session=1297194043D4F.19234&limitbox_2=TM
01+%3D+tm_b01&menu=search&aspect=subtab124&npp=50&ipp=20&spp=20&profile=bib&
ri=8&source=~!horizon&index=.TW&term=defamation+of+religions&x=0&y=0&aspect=subta
b124#focus. The OIC will be further considered in Chapter Nine.

195 UN Human Rights Council Resolution proposed by, among others, Pakistan on behalf of the Organization of the Islamic Conference. A/HRC/10/L.2/Rev.1, passed on March 26, 2009

196 Id.

197 Available online at www.oic-un.org/document_report/Islamophobia_rep_May_23_25_2009.pdf

198 Second Observatory Report on Islamophobia, p. 8

Journalistic associations have long enshrined freedom of the press in their statements of principles. The Associated Press Managing Editors' *Statement of Ethical Principles,* adopted in 1994, declares that, "The newspaper and its staff should be free of obligations to news sources and newsmakers. Even the appearance of obligation or conflict of interest should be avoided."[199]

Similarly, the American Society of News Editors' *Statement of Principles* stresses journalistic independence and states that "they must be vigilant against all who would exploit the press for selfish purposes."[200] The Radio Television Digital News Association's *Code of Ethics and Professional Conduct* not only calls for journalists to "resist those who would seek to buy or politically influence news content" but also to recognize "that any professional or government licensing of journalists is a violation of that freedom."[201]

Still, the codification of journalistic self-censorship has already begun in some circles. The Society of Professional Journalists (SPJ) passed a resolution on October 6, 2001, shortly after the terrorist attack on 9/11, that urged journalists not only to avoid using "inflammatory" language, but also included a series of directives concerning the portrayal of Islam and Muslims, even calling for journalists to "ask men and women from within targeted communities to review your coverage and make suggestions."[202] This in spite of the SPJ's own previously adopted,

---

199 Ethics Statement, Associated Press Managing Editors,
http://www.apme.com/?page=EthicsStatement (last visited Nov. 24, 2010).
200 ASNE's Statement of Principles, ASNE (Aug. 27, 2009),
http://asne.org/article_view/smid/370/articleid/325/reftab/79/t/asnes-statement-of-principles.aspx.
201 Code of Ethics and Professional Conduct, RTDNA,
http://www.rtdna.org/pages/media_items/code-of-ethics-and-professional-conduct48.php (last visited Nov. 24, 2010).
202 Guidelines for Countering Racial, Ethic and Religious Profiling, Soc'y of Prof. Journalists,

and still extant, ethical guideline that "journalists should be free of obligation to any interest other than the public's right to know."[203]

We are forced to question, why is the SPJ singling out Islam for preferential treatment as a particularly sensitive topic? What is a "targeted community?" Is the SPJ even qualified to state that "[t]he basic meaning of 'jihad' is to exert oneself for the good of Islam and to better oneself,"[204] particularly when the term unquestionably has another, violent meaning?[205] Above all, do we really live in an era when investigative reporting on how religion is used to justify violence is somehow no longer responsible absent some sort of prior-review or approval from the community?

Also of concern are the principles guiding the Accrediting Council on Education in Journalism and Mass Communications (ACEJMC), "the agency responsible for the evaluation of professional journalism and mass communications programs in colleges and universities."[206] The ACEJMC's Accrediting Standards preamble ends with the following:

> ACEJMC will apply its standards and indicators in compliance with applicable laws and regulations and, where appropriate, with *religious or cultural prescriptions and practices.*[207] [Emphasis added]

---

http://www.spj.org/divguidelines.asp (last visited Nov. 24, 2010).

203 SJP Code of Ethics, Soc'y of Prof. Journalists, http://www.spj.org/ethicscode.asp (last visited Nov. 24, 2010). http://www.spj.org/divguidelines.asp

204 Id

205 Traditionally, jihad has been understood in Islamic law to include a military effort that is a religious obligation on the Muslim community as a whole and against non-believers of the Islamic faith. A person engaged in jihad is called a *mujahid*, the plural is *mujahideen.*

206 ACEJMC Homepage, http://www2.ku.edu/~acejmc/ (last visited Nov. 24, 2010).

207 Accrediting Standards, ACEJMC, http://www2.ku.edu/~acejmc/PROGRAM/STANDARDS.SHTML (last visited Nov. 24, 2010) (emphasis added).

While the ACEJMC's intent to accommodate a wide range of cultural and religious orientations may be worthy, what happens when a religious segment demands standards that effectively circumscribe reporting objectively? This is precisely the sort of standard proponents of censorship look to exploit.

While the OIC's attempts to redefine freedom of speech and the press will receive a fuller treatment in Chapter Nine, it is important to note that the OIC adopted the Cairo Declaration of Human Rights in Islam[208] decades after the Universal Declaration of Human Rights was codified. The Cairo Declaration, enacted in 1990, mentions the right to express an opinion, but only "in such manner as would not be contrary to the principles of the Shari'ah."[209] Similarly, information itself "may not be exploited or misused in such a way as may violate sanctities and the dignity of Prophets..." When a western media organization like ACEJMC requires "compliance with religious practices" for reporting on campuses, it imposes an unacceptable dilemma, where writers may be advised, pressured or even forced to censor themselves according to standards defined by groups like the OIC.

---

208 See Appendix D.
209 Id.

9

THE ORGANIZATION OF ISLAMIC COOPERATION AND THE SUBVERSION OF FREE SPEECH

" We cannot and should not be oblivious of world opinion but we certainly ought to be as attentive to what we have to say to the world as to what the world has to say to or for us. We must not permit the prejudiced and ignorant to shape our lives. The prejudiced will always call the best worst and the ignorant will confuse the two."

U.S. SUPREME COURT JUSTICE LOUIS D. BRANDEIS [210]

" [U]ttering profanities against Prophet Muhammad (PBUH) is the worst form of human rights violation in the world. Attacks on the values and tenets of Islam are extremely dangerous and unacceptable."

DR. ADEL AL-DAMKHI, CHAIRMAN OF THE KUWAIT HUMAN RIGHTS SOCIETY [211]

---

210 Cited in The Words of Justice Brandeis 47 (Solomon Goldman ed. 1953).

211 'YouTube' Must Erase Anti-Islam Material: KHRS, Arab Times (Oct. 2, 2008), available at http://europenews.dk/en/node/14648.

U.S. Supreme Court Justice Hugo Black once observed that, "No purpose in ratifying the Bill of Rights was clearer than that of securing for the people of the United States much greater freedom of religion, expression, assembly, and petition than the people of Great Britain had ever enjoyed."[212] Indeed, the protections afforded freedom of speech and of the press in the United States remain, in many ways, uniquely progressive nearly two and a half centuries since the 1776 state constitutions of Virginia and North Carolina termed freedom of the press "one of the great bulwarks of liberty,"[213] and Pennsylvania's contemporaneous Bill of Rights affirmed "That the people have a right to freedom of speech, and of writing, and publishing their sentiments; therefore the freedom of the press ought not to be restrained."[214]

These rights are by no means exclusive to Americans, of course. On December 10, 1948, the United Nations General Assembly adopted the Universal Declaration of Human Rights (UDHR), which recognized that the "highest aspiration of the common people" was to see "a world in which human beings shall enjoy freedom of speech and belief and freedom from fear and want."[215] The UDHR explicitly outlined this inherent human *right* in Article 19 wherein it is declared that, "Everyone has the right to freedom of opinion and expression; this right includes freedom to hold opinions without interference and to seek, receive and impart information and ideas through any media and regardless of frontiers." The inherent right to free speech includes the right to promote opinions regarding issues of public concern including

---

212 Bridges v. California, 314 U.S. 252, 265 (1941).

213 Section 12 and point 15 thereof, respectively.

214 Right XII

215 Available online at http://www.un.org/en/documents/udhr/index.shtml

religious extremism. When the teachings of a religion are being used to justify terrorism, and critical analysis of the issue is suppressed in deference to a political body, the right to freely hold opinions and impart information is rendered toothless.

After lengthy deliberation, the UN General Assembly adopted two international covenants in 1966 that built upon the UDHR, the International Covenant on Economic, Social and Cultural Rights[216] (ICESCR) and the International Covenant on Civil and Political Rights[217] (ICCPR). Article 19 of the ICCPR deals with rights enshrined in the UDHR, but notably qualifies that the exercise of the right to freedom of expression "carries with it special duties and responsibilities [and] may therefore be subject to certain restrictions." While the elucidation of the right is set forth differently from American First Amendment case law, the specific restrictions listed in Article 19 are limited to protecting the "respect of the rights or reputations of others" and "national security or of public order (*ordre public*), or of public health or morals."

Although not entirely contiguous with the American tradition, these categories may be construed to accord with two traditional exceptions to free speech protection within the United States, obscenity and defamation (neither of which is protected speech under the Constitution) though the U.S. explicitly declared upon signing ICCPR that:

> For the United States, article 5, paragraph 2, which provides that fundamental human rights existing in any State Party may not be diminished on the pretext that the Covenant recognizes them to a lesser extent, has particular

---

216 Available online at http://www2.ohchr.org/english/law/cescr.htm
217 Available online at http://www2.ohchr.org/english/law/ccpr.htm

relevance to article 19, paragraph 3 which would permit certain restrictions on the freedom of expression. The United States declares that it will continue to adhere to the requirements and constraints of its Constitution in respect to all such restrictions and limitations.[218]

ICCPR's Article 20 is another matter entirely. It expressly prohibits "Any propaganda for war" as well as "Any advocacy of national, racial or religious hatred that constitutes incitement to discrimination, hostility or violence." When the U.S. signed ICCPR, it did so with several reservations, including "That article 20 does not authorize or require legislation or other action by the United States that would restrict the right of free speech and association protected by the Constitution and laws of the United States."[219] This reservation reflected the fact that in the U.S., treaties cannot supersede or contradict the Constitution. As the Supreme Court has noted, "[t]his Court has regularly and uniformly recognized the supremacy of the Constitution over a treaty."[220]

These differences in interpretation of the scope of free speech might, in other contexts, be relatively minor and best suited for academic discussion. There are numerous nations and political interest groups that define the core freedom very differently, however, and are seeking to alter the international norms to suit their worldview.

The Organization of Islamic Cooperation is a 57-member[221] entity that comprises "the second largest inter-

---

218 http://treaties.un.org/Pages/ViewDetails.aspx?src=TREATY&mtdsg_no=IV-4&chapter=4&lang=en#EndDec

219 "U.S. reservations, declarations, and understandings, International Covenant on Civil and Political Rights," 138 Cong. Rec. S4781-01 (daily ed., April 2, 1992).

220 Reid v. Covert, 341 U.S. 1, 17 (1957)

221 The number 57 includes the 'state' of Palestine. http://www.oic-oci.org/member_states.asp

governmental organization after the United Nations" and claims to represent "the collective voice of the Muslim world."[222] As UN watchdog Eye on the UN[223] has pointed out, "The OIC is the largest single subset of both the G-77 and the NAM [Non-Aligned Movement]." The G-77 is a voting bloc of 131[224] third-world nations and China, which constitutes approximately 68% of the UN General Assembly.[225] The NAM bloc is comprised of 118[226] nations, or approximately 61% of the General Assembly.

While generally paying lip service to UDHR, the OIC is bound by the *Cairo Declaration on Human Rights in Islam*.[227] Enacted by the OIC in 1990, the *Cairo Declaration* does mention a right to express an opinion, but only so long as it is expressed "in such manner as would not be contrary to the principles of the Shari'ah." Similarly, information, though a "vital necessity," "may not be exploited or misused in such a way as may violate sanctities and the dignity of Prophets..." Obviously, such restrictions render the enumerated rights subservient to religious doctrine.

Islam includes several main schools of Shi'a and Sunni jurisprudence, which are in broad agreement about the majority of tenets contained in Shariah law. Shariah law is derived primarily from the Qur'an and the Sunna (plus *ijma*, or consensus of the scholars, and *qiyas*, or reasoning by analogy). The Sunna comprises Muhammad's biography (the *Sira*) and several authoritative collections of the actions and sayings of Muhammad,

---

222 About OIC, Org. of the Islamic Conf., http://www.oic-oci.org/page_detail.asp?p_id=52

223 Political Alliances Within the UN, Eye on the UN,
http://www.eyeontheun.org/view.asp?l=11&p=55 (last visited Nov. 24, 2010).

224 http://www.g77.org/doc/members.html

225 The UN has 192 member states. http://www.un.org/depts/dhl/unms/whatisms.shtml#states

226
http://www.namegypt.org/en/AboutName/MembersObserversAndGuests/Pages/default.aspx

227 See Appendix D.

known as *ahadith*.[228] In the *ahadith* deemed authoritative by the scholars of Sunni Islam, there are sayings that have been found to justify the deadly suppression of any speech critical of Muhammad. One of the six most authoritative *ahadith* is *Sunan Abu Dawud*, written in the 9th Century, CE. It contains a very troubling account, "Narrated Ali ibn Abu Talib: A Jewess used to abuse the Prophet (peace be upon him) and disparage him. A man strangled her till she died. The Apostle of Allah (peace be upon him) declared that no recompense was payable for her blood."[229] In other words, the murder of a woman for insulting Muhammad did not merit even monetary compensation.

While there are non-authoritative trends within the popular practice of Islam that do not seek to impose or even allow such draconian punishments for "abusing" or "defaming" any religious figure, the OIC has embarked on a campaign spread over a decade that seeks to globally criminalize "defamation of religion." As noted in Chapter Eight, since 1999, the OIC has introduced and lobbied for the passage of at least 18[230] non-binding resolutions at the United Nations General Assembly and Human Rights Council that have called for what amounts to a wholesale revision of international free speech rights in order specifically to protect Islam.

For example, the UN Human Rights Council resolution A/HRC/10/L.2/Rev.1, Combating defamation of religions,[231]

---

228 Hadith, the more familiar term, is the singular form.
229 Sunan Abu Dawud 38:4349.
230
http://unbisnet.un.org:8080/ipac20/ipac.jsp?session=1297194043D4F.19234&limitbox_2=TM
01+%3D+tm_b01&menu=search&aspect=subtab124&npp=50&ipp=20&spp=20&profile=bib&
ri=8&source=~!horizon&index=.TW&term=defamation+of+religions&x=0&y=0&aspect=subta
b124#focus
231 http://www.unitedstatesaction.com/documents/A-HRC-10-L.2-Rev.1--March-2009.doc

which passed on March, 26, 2009, expressed concern over "the need to effectively combat defamation of all religions and incitement to religious hatred in general *and against Islam and Muslims in particular*" [Emphasis added] and further requested that the applicable UN Special Rapporteur report on defamation of religion "and in particular on the serious implications of Islamophobia." This was a more nuanced version of an argument set forth in the first "Defamation of Religion" resolution which expressed singular concern "that Islam is frequently and wrongly associated with human rights violations and with terrorism."[232] What are the chances that these resolutions will be used to condemn terrorist groups that kill in the name of Islam?

While the OIC has attempted to portray its campaign as reflecting the consensus of a broad range of countries "beyond the membership of the OIC,"[233] a number of countries and non-governmental organizations from around the world have voiced grave concerns with the OIC's maneuvering. In fact, UN Special Rapporteur on Freedom of Expression Frank la Rue voiced his opposition to the campaign in 2009, arguing that "[r]estrictions should never be used to protect particular institutions or abstract notions, concepts or beliefs, including religious ones."[234] This prompted an attack by Pakistan (on behalf of the OIC) and Egypt (on behalf of the African Group), which

---

232 "Defamation of Religions" E/CN.4/RES/1999/82, adopted by the UN Commission on Human Rights without a vote, Apr. 30, 1999.
http://ap.ohchr.org/documents/E/CHR/resolutions/E-CN_4-RES-1999-82.doc

233 OIC Clarifies Its Views on the Draft Resolution on Combating Defamation of Religions, Org. of the Islamic Conf. (Feb. 11, 2009), http://www.oic-oci.org/topic_detail.asp?t_id=2922.

234 Deutsche-Presse Agentur, Islamic States Clash with UN Expert on Free Speech, Earth Times News (June 3, 2009), http://www.earthtimes.org/articles/news/271545,islamic-states-clash-with-un-expert-on-free-speech.html

admonished la Rue for focusing on protecting freedom of expression, rather than reporting on "abuses of this freedom."[235]

Recently, others have begun objecting to the resolutions. In June 2008, the European Centre for Law and Justice submitted a comprehensive legal critique of UN Resolution 7/19[236] to the UN Office of the High Commissioner of Human Rights.[237] More recently, on November 12, 2009, the Center for Security Policy was among over 100 non-governmental organizations from around the world that signed a joint statement,[238] describing the United Nations resolutions on the `defamation of religions' as "incompatible with the fundamental freedoms of individuals to freely exercise and peacefully express their thoughts, ideas, and beliefs."

The OIC's response to criticisms levied against its anti-free speech campaign has been to brand its critics as "Islam-ophobes," bemoaning alleged 'smear campaigns' "by some NGOs as well as lobby and interest groups in the West on baseless presumptions aimed at misleading the Western public opinion."[239] In point of fact, the OIC's refusal to respond to the numerous critics of its campaign in favor of attacking the critics themselves is nothing less than a global *ad hominem* campaign "marked by... an attack on an opponent's character rather than by an answer to the contentions made."[240] It is also presumptuous for the OIC to

---

235 Id

236 The 2008 Human Rights Council iteration of the resolution, A/HRC/Res/7/19, adopted March 27, 2008.

237 Available online at
http://www.meforum.org/pics/ECLJ_submission_to_OHCHR_on_Combating_Defamation_of_Religions.pdf

238 Available online at http://whatisdefamationofreligion.com/

239 http://www.oic-oci.org/topic_detail.asp?t_id=2922

240 "ad hominem." Merriam-Webster Online Dictionary. 2010. Available online at http://www.merriam-webster.com/dictionary/ad+hominem

attack people defending their rights to free speech, rights which have been fought and paid for by the blood of their countrymen, and freedoms which are not enjoyed in the majority of OIC states.

Sadly, even the US, under the Obama administration, has been lulled into assisting the OIC's attack on freedom of speech, such as by the September 2009 Human Rights Council resolution on Freedom of opinion and expression[241] introduced jointly by the United States and Egypt—even if accompanied by a critique[242] of the religious defamation campaign by the US Secretary of State. The resolution itself seems clearly in conflict with the US Constitution,[243] yet that is not the most dangerous aspect of facilitating the OIC's campaign.

Resolutions passed by the Human Rights Council and even its General Assembly *are not binding, enforceable laws.* So why has the OIC spent over 10 years passing a series of near-identical resolutions?

The answer lies in what is called "customary international law." At its most basic, "customary international law develops from the practice of States."[244] It may be defined as "rules of law derived

---

241 http://ap.ohchr.org/documents/E/HRC/d_res_dec/A_HRC_12_L14.doc

242 http://www.state.gov/secretary/rm/2009a/10/130937.htm

243 See E.G., Law Professor Jonathan Turley, Just Say No To Blasphemy: U.S. Supports Egypt In Limiting Anti-Religious Speech, USA Today, October 18, 2009. The Original Article Is Not Available At The Newspaper's Website, But Is Available At The Author's Site At Http://Jonathanturley.Org/2009/10/19/Just-Say-No-To-Blasphemy-U-S-Supports-Eygpt-In-Limiting-Anti-Religious-Speech; And Eugene Volokh, Is The Obama Administration Supporting Calls To Outlaw Supposed Hate Speech?, The Volokh Conspiracy, October 1, 2009, In Which He Expresses Concern "That It [The Us/Egyptian Resolution] Might Be A Step Backward For Our Own Constitutional Rights, Because Of What Seems To Be The U.S. Endorsement Of The Suppression Of "Any Advocacy Of National, Racial Or Religious Hatred That Constitutes Incitement To Discrimination, Hostility Or Violence" And Possibly Of "Negative Stereotyping Of Religions And Racial Groups." Http://Volokh.Com/2009/10/01/Is-The-Obama-Administration-Supporting-Calls-To-Suppress-Supposed-Hate-Speech/

244 Thomas Buergenthal and Harold G. Maier, Public International Law in a Nutshell, 3d Ed., West Group 2002, pp. 22-23

from the consistent conduct of States acting out of the belief that the law required them to act that way."[245] While the precise nature and extent of customary international law are well beyond the scope of this book, it is no mere abstraction. For example, Article 38 of the Statute of the International Court of Justice provides that the Court shall apply "international custom, as evidence of a general practice accepted as law."[246]

As law professor Ilya Somin warned:

[I]t is likely that international human rights law, as currently developed, does more to legitimize repression than to protect freedom. This is especially likely in light of the fact that repressive regimes can usually disobey those aspects of such law that might genuinely weaken their grip on power. By contrast, liberal democratic states are likely to take the rule of law more seriously and therefore to actually obey repressive elements of human rights treaties that they ratify and commit to incorporating into their domestic law.[247]

Ultimately, the OIC, along with other Islamist organizations and individuals, is attempting to define a new international custom and practice, not a balance between freedom of opinion and respect for all religions. Hence, the OIC is maneuvering to create precedents in international law that can be used to justify the suppression of public dialogue, in the West and elsewhere, about matters that pertain in any way to Islam, from open

---

245 Shabtai Rosenne, Practice and Methods of International Law, Oceana New York 1984, p. 55.
246 Article 38(b). Available online at http://www.icj-cij.org/documents/index.php?p1=4&p2=2&p3=0
247 How the Recent UN Human Rights Council Resolution on Freedom of Speech Exemplifies the Dangers of Authoritarian Regimes' Influence over International Law, The Volokh Conspiracy, November 1, 2009. http://volokh.com/2009/11/01/the-un-human-rights-council-resolution-and-the-flaws-of-international-human-rights-law/

discussion on terrorism to the acceptability of criticizing even radical forms of Islam. For this reason, "we should view the current body of law in this area with great suspicion, and be very reluctant to allow it to override or influence the domestic law of liberal democracies."[248]

As the following chapter illustrates, the next battleground over freedom of expression is the newest and most fertile ground for the dissemination of information the world has ever seen—the Internet.

---

248 Id.

10

DEFAMATION AND THE INTERNET:
SPECIAL CONSIDERATIONS

"As the most participatory form of mass speech yet developed, the Internet deserves the highest protection from governmental intrusion.... Just as the strength of the Internet is chaos, so the strength of our liberty depends upon the chaos and cacophony of the unfettered speech the First Amendment protects."

DISTRICT COURT, EASTERN PENNSYLVANIA,
ACLU v. RENO [249]

A legal question that faced American courts for decades was whether, in a defamation case, multiple copies of a book or of a newspaper each constituted a separate act of publication (and therefore multiple acts of defamation), or if multiple copies of the same text should be considered one publication. The courts recognized that allowing separate causes of action for each copy of a publication could lead to endless liability and absurd results at law.

---

249 929 F.Supp. 824, 883 (E.D. Pa. 1996)

As early as 1938, New York courts ruled that multiple copies would only give rise to a single cause of action for defamation even if a publisher were to hold onto unsold copies of a defamatory work for 20 years,[250] and in 1948 extended the rule to cover books as well as periodicals.[251] Thus, while new *editions*, such as morning and evening newspapers or hard- and soft-cover books could form the basis for multiple defamation claims, multiple *copies* of the same publication could not. This became known as the single publication rule.

The Internet added a new dimension for courts to consider. Since web pages are constantly updated, courts had to face the question of whether each updated web page constituted a new publication for the purposes of a defamation claim. In 2002, the New York Court of Appeals ruled that Internet websites were subject to the single publication rule, even if the webpage were modified slightly after the initial publication,[252] and that failing to apply the rule would inhibit free exchange of ideas on the Internet. In other words, the Court decided not to treat an updated web page as a new edition. Some, but not all, states have followed New York's lead.

Still, as Internet law continues to develop, there are several issues of which Internet journalists need to be aware, which are addressed briefly in this chapter.

Unlike traditional forms of media, anything published on the Internet is accessible virtually anywhere, leading to potential exposure in multiple jurisdictions. In an article recommending

---

250 Wolfson v. Syracuse Newspapers, Inc., 254 A.D. 211 (4th Dep't 1938), affirmed without opinion by 279 N.Y. 716 (1939)

251 Gregoire v. G.P. Putnam's Sons, 298 N.Y. 119 (1948)

252 Firth v. State, 98 N.Y.2d 365 (2002)

that bloggers secure media insurance, director of the Citizen Media Law Project, David Ardia, explained:

> Here is a simple, but often ignored, truth: if you publish online, whether it's a news article, blog post, podcast, video, or even a user comment, you open yourself up to potential legal liability. It doesn't matter whether you are a professional journalist, hockey-mom, or an obscure blogger, if you post it, you'll need to be prepared for the legal consequences.[253]

Within the United States, there have already been several cases in which local newspapers have been sued by parties thousands of miles away on the basis of an article uploaded to the Internet. Such was the case in *Young v. New Haven Advocate*,[254] in which the warden of a Virginia prison unsuccessfully sued two Connecticut-based newspapers for reporting critically on how prisoners from Connecticut were treated while housed in the Virginia warden's prison. In *Young*, the Court held that since the newspapers directed their articles to readers based in Connecticut and had not manifested an intent to target Virginia readers, the mere fact that the article could be read in Virginia was insufficient to allow the plaintiff to sue in a Virginia court. In other words, the Court looked at the target audience of the article rather than whether it was accessible elsewhere via the Internet.

When publishing on the Internet about events and figures that transcend national boundaries, however, journalists may expose themselves to some degree of liability in another country,

---

253 "New Insurance Program for Bloggers Offered by the Media Bloggers Association," Citizen Media Law Project, September 23, 2008. Available online at
http://www.citmedialaw.org/blog/2008/new-insurance-program-bloggers-offered-media-bloggers-association
254 315 F.3d 256 (4th Cir. 2002)

and the foreign laws that may apply are likely to offer less protection for speech compared to the laws of the United States.

Republishing an article may create a similar problem in terms of liability, as Ravindra Kumar and Anand Sinha of the Calcutta, India *Statesman* discovered when they republished an article from the United Kingdom-based *Independent*, entitled "Why should I respect these oppressive religions?" by Johann Hari.[255] The Hari article, which appeared in the *Independent*'s print and online editions, dealt with the growing inability to criticize all religions, including, but not limited to, Islam.

After the *Statesman* republished the article, it was met by Muslim protests and a police complaint alleging that the article had 'outraged religious feelings.' Kumar and Sinha, editor and publisher of the newspaper, were arrested under Indian laws criminalizing the incitement of hatred against religion, though they were later released from jail and apologized.[256] And even though Hari was not charged in the U.K. under its own hate speech laws, and had nothing to do with the republication, he noted that "I am told I too will be arrested if I go to Calcutta."[257]

In what has been an anomalous case, an Australian court held in 2002 that Internet defamation occurs in whatever jurisdiction the article is downloaded.[258] While even Australian courts have not subsequently relied on the 2002 ruling, an

---

255 Originally published by the Independent January 28, 2009, it remains available online at http://www.independent.co.uk/opinion/commentators/johann-hari/johann-hari-why-should-i-respect-these-oppressive-religions-1517789.html

256 Jerome Taylor, Editor arrested for 'outraging Muslims,' The Independent, February 12, 2009. http://www.independent.co.uk/news/world/asia/editor-arrested-for-outraging-muslims-1607256.html

257 "Johann Hari: Despite these riots, I stand by what I wrote," the Independent, February 13, 2009. Available online at http://www.independent.co.uk/opinion/commentators/johann-hari/johann-hari-despite-these-riots-i-stand-by-what-i-wrote-1608059.html

258 Dow Jones & Company v. Gutnick, (2002) 210 C.L.R. 575

Australian political faction has been pushing for a mandatory Internet filter that would effectively censor the Internet , under the guise of protecting users from "child pornography and adult content."[259]

For journalists writing in the United States, the possibility of being exposed to foreign liability for articles posted to the Internet, or even books sold over the Internet, is no small matter. The United Kingdom is a favored ground for predatory lawsuits alleging libel, due to the UK's plaintiff-friendly defamation laws. [260]

The late Saudi billionaire Khalid bin Mahfouz was dubbed "the libel tourist" after he sued or threatened to sue *more than 30* publishers and authors in British courts, including several Americans, whose written works have linked him to terrorist entities. In 2003, anti-terrorism analyst and director of the American Center for Democracy, Dr. Rachel Ehrenfeld, published a book entitled, *Funding Evil: How Terrorism Is Financed—and How to Stop It*, in which she alleged financial ties between wealthy Saudis, including Mahfouz, and terrorist entities such as al Qaeda. Mahfouz sued Ehrenfeld for defamation in the UK, and a UK court chose to hear the case despite the fact that neither Mahfouz nor Ehrenfeld resides in England and merely because approximately 23 copies of *Funding Evil* were sold online to UK buyers via Amazon.com.[261]

---

259 "Australia to implement mandatory Internet censorship," the Herald Sun, October 29, 2008. Available online at http://www.heraldsun.com.au/news/mandatory-censorship-on-web/story-0-1111117883306

260 The authors wrote and circulated brief memorandum highlighting pertinent differences between US and UK libel to members of Parliament and Congress in December 2008. The memorandum may be found in Appendix C, and is available online at http://www.legal-project.com/documents/221.doc

261 Douglas Lee, 2 international libel cases could benefit U.S. publishers, First Amendment Center Online, October 18, 2005. http://www.firstamendmentcenter.org/analysis.aspx?id=15940

Though Ehrenfeld lost the UK case by default after refusing to travel to England and recognize the court's jurisdiction, she was able to convince first New York lawmakers and eventually Congress, that US-based journalists must be protected against such libel tourism suits. In response, New York passed the Libel Terrorism Protection Act[262] in 2008, followed by the enactment of the federal Securing and Protecting our Enduring and Established Constitutional Heritage Act[263] (SPEECH Act) in 2010. In general, such laws work to nullify foreign libel judgments against American authors obtained in jurisdictions with lesser free speech protections, and cases that would otherwise not succeed in American courts.

Further emerging areas of concern include websites like bit.ly, which provide a service that shortens Internet addresses for social networking sites such as Twitter. Generally, every country can host web pages through a suffix, or "extension" relating to the country, known as a "country code Top Level Domain" or ccTLD. The United States has the ccTLD .us, for example. The .ly ccTLD belongs to Libya, whose terms of use[264] state that registrants must attest that "the domain name is not being registered for any activities/purpose not permitted under Libyan law." In 2010, Libya deleted the domain "vb.ly" for allegedly failing to comply with Libyan law, prompting the domain's owner to warn that ".ly domains deemed to be in violation of NIC.ly regulation are being deregistered and removed without warning—causing significant inconvenience and damage" and that "Libyan Islamic/Sharia Law

---

262 Originally introduced in the New York State Assembly and State Senate as A.9652 and S.6687, respectively.

263 H.R. 2765. http://www.gpo.gov/fdsys/pkg/BILLS-111hr2765enr/pdf/BILLS-111hr2765enr.pdf

264 Available online at http://nic.ly/regulations.php

is being used to consider the validity of domains, which is unclear and obscure in terms of being able to know what is allowed and what isn't."[265]

Still another lawfare issue that has been largely resolved lies in protections afforded Internet service providers. During the late 1990s, Internet service provider America Online maintained online chat rooms, some of which were meant for discussion on Islam, entitled "Koran" and "Beliefs: Islam." Saad Noah, a user of the chat rooms, filed suit against AOL over remarks he deemed to be offensive to Islam, claiming that the remarks constituted 'harassment' under the US Civil Rights Act of 1964. AOL moved to dismiss the case, and the Court agreed, stating that allowing such a suit would be contrary to the purpose of the Internet as a "forum for true diversity of political discourse, unique opportunities for cultural development, and myriad avenues for intellectual activity."[266] Noah appealed to the Fourth Circuit Court of Appeals, which affirmed the lower court in an unpublished per curiam opinion.[267]

In fact, *Noah* followed the logic of prior opinions regarding the non-liability of Internet Service Providers and third-party content. In 1997, the Fourth Circuit Court of Appeals held that America Online, as an Internet service provider (ISP), could be not be held liable for allegedly defamatory statements that appeared on an AOL bulletin board and which were posted by third parties.[268] The Court's ruling rested on the Communications Decency Act of 1996, which states "No provider or user of an

---

265 Ben Metcalf, The .ly domain space to be considered unsafe, Ben Metcalf Blog, October 6, 2010.

266 Noah v. AOL Time Warner, 261 F.Supp.2d 532, 538 (E.D.Va. 2003)

267 Noah v. AOL Time Warner, No. 03-1770 (4th Cir. March 24, 2004)

268 Zeran v. American Online, Inc., 129 F3d 327 (4th Cir. 1997)

interactive computer service shall be treated as the publisher or speaker of any information provided by another information content provider."[269] That is, if person A posts a comment on AOL's site, AOL, being an ISP, can not be held liable for the content of person A's publication. This makes perfect sense when one considers the ramifications if the rule was otherwise, requiring providers to act like speech police over the thousands of people posting on their sites.

This, however, is another area where protections taken for granted in the United States may not be available in other countries.

Harry's Place[270] is a blog that seeks to be one of "the few blogs...to offer a democratic-left perspective."[271] In 2008, Harry's Place ran an article that posted a translated transcription of speech made in the course of an *Al Jazeera* interview with Mohammad Sawalha, president of the British Muslim Initiative.[272] In *Al Jazeera*'s initial transcript of the interview, Sawalha referenced the "Jewish evil" in Britain, and Harry's Place posted the original transcript to its site. Later on, *Al Jazeera* claimed the interview had been mis-transcribed and replaced the word "evil" with "lobby." After the change, Harry's Place noted that the *Al Jazeera* transcript had been altered, but refused a demand by Sawalha that the article be taken down in its entirety. Harry's Place was then sent a threatening legal letter on Sawalha's behalf.[273] As Harry's Place remained defiant, Sawalha eventually dropped his complaint

---

269 47 U.S.C. § 230(c)(1)

270 http://www.hurryupharry.org

271 "This is HP," available online at http://www.hurryupharry.org/about/

272 "British Muslim Initiative: We Resent the Evil Jew in Britain" by David T, July 2, 2008. Available online at http://www.hurryupharry.org/2008/07/02/british-muslim-initiative-we-resent-the-evil-jew-in-britain/

273 Id, see "Update" section of the above article

against the blog and the article remains available on its website. On the other hand, when Sawalha sued the British *Spectator* newspaper and journalist Melanie Phillips for reporting on the same story, the case was eventually settled, and in exchange for dropping his complaint, the defendants issued an apology and paid Sawalha's court costs.[274]

A unique issue that arises from blogs lies in their essentially hybrid nature. Many blogs are not precisely media in traditional terms, they are not written by experienced journalists, nor are they mass marketed publications. Yet blogs often perform an important function customarily held by media, that is, the public dissemination of timely and newsworthy information.

In the case against Joe Kaufman mentioned in Chapters Two and Six, the Texas Court of Appeals found Kaufman to be a member of the media because his articles appeared on the electronic publication Front Page Magazine,[275] which exercised editorial control in a fashion similar to traditional newspaper publications, and because Kaufman had journalistic training. Had Kaufman not been an investigative reporter, but 'merely' a blogger, he may not have been able to make use of the motion that won his case. Accordingly, bloggers not operating as part of the traditional "mainstream media" should be aware that their rights as members of the press have not yet been fully delineated by courts, and they may or may not be afforded the same protections as traditional journalists.

While newspapers and other traditional media are generally covered by media insurance policies, most if not all

---

274 Josh Halliday, The Spectator apologises for falsely accusing Muslim of anti-Semitism, The Guardian, November 25, 2010. http://www.guardian.co.uk/media/2010/nov/25/spectator-apology-muslim-antisemitism

275 http://frontpagemag.com/

bloggers do not obtain insurance even though they may be writing about controversial issues. For this reason, the Media Bloggers Association created a new educational, advisory and insurance program for bloggers in September 2008.[276] In a similar vein, News University recently introduced an online course for bloggers entitled "Online Media Law: The Basics for Bloggers and Other Publishers."[277] As a practical matter, the authors of this book highly recommend that bloggers writing about Islam, terrorism and their sources of financing secure media insurance and continue to educate themselves about this developing area of law.

The unique and unprecedented connection between the Internet and freedom of expression, including freedom of the press, continues to be examined, and likely will take unexpected turns. After Egypt blocked all domestic Internet access for a week amid protests in early 2011, many decried the action as a violation of human rights, with attorney David Tafuri explicitly stating that "Internet blackout is a freedom blackout—an assault on fundamental and inalienable rights to freedom of expression, assembly and press."[278] Though it is too soon to predict how the Internet will fully affect existing free expression norms, the fact that Egypt's Internet shutdown was an abject failure on many

276 "Media Bloggers Association Launches Education, Legal Advisory And Liability Insurance Program For Bloggers," Media Bloggers Association Press Release, September 18, 2008. Available online at http://www.mediabloggers.org/mba-announcement/media-bloggers-association-launches-education-legal-advisory-and-liability-insurance-program-for-bloggers

277 Course Details available online at
http://www.newsu.org/courses/course_detail.aspx?id=nwsu_medialaw08

278 Egypt's Assault on the World-Wide Web, The Wall Street Journal, February 9, 2011.
http://online.wsj.com/article/SB10001424052748704858404576128700182910370.html?KEY
WORDS=egypt's+assault

levels[279] gives every reason to hope that we will see more protection for these rights, not less.

---

279 See, e.g. Wayne Rash, Egyptian Internet Shutdown Batters Economy, Fails to Quell Protests, eWeek.com, February 1, 2011. http://www.eweek.com/c/a/IT-Infrastructure/Egyptian-Internet-Shutdown-Batters-Economy-Fails-to-Quell-Protests-640505/

11

CONCLUSION

" The security of the nation is not at the ramparts alone. Security also lies in the value of our free institutions. A cantankerous press, an obstinate press, an ubiquitous press must be suffered by those in authority in order to preserve the even greater values of freedom of expression and the right of the people to know."

UNITED STATES V. NEW YORK TIMES CO.[280]

The course of American history has always rested in large part on an active populace, informed by a free and robust press. These principles are no less important today. Much as Judge Gurfein stated in the above quote, when lawfare targets open discourse on religion, its use to justify terrorism and terrorism's sources of funding, the ramparts in the fight to secure free speech are not merely overseas, but here as well. And just as the First Amendment ensures that our government may not abridge the freedoms of speech and of the press, so too must we not allow foreign powers, or the cumulative effect of individual

---

280 328 F.Supp. 324, 331 (S.D.N.Y. 1971) The trial court's ruling was eventually affirmed by the United States Supreme Court in New York Times Co. v. United States, 403 U.S. 713 (1971)

lawsuits, to turn our legal institutions against the very rights they are meant to protect.

It is true that journalists, bloggers or anyone reporting on controversial topics may be exposed to attack through use of legal processes, especially once the tactic has proven successful at stifling dialogue. Some of the tactics mentioned in this book likely will appear again, whether in the Islamist lawfare context or in a completely different scenario. And while Islamists' use of libel tourism dropped precipitously since the demise of Khalid bin Mahfouz, there have been recent attempts to bring UK libel suits against several Danish newspapers[281] and the intrepid president of the American Islamic Forum for Democracy, Dr. M. Zuhdi Jasser.[282]

Though this might appear to be cause for alarm, the fact is that both attempts to resurrect libel tourism have met with decisive and immediate reaction, with a Danish ministerial complaint to the European Commission[283] and the unanimous passing of protective legislation by the Arizona Senate[284] respectively. And on August 10, 2010, the President signed into law a federal Speech Act,[285] which states as a matter of law that "a domestic court shall not recognize or enforce a foreign judgment

---

281 "Saudi lawyer uses English libel to sue Danish papers," MediaWatchWatch, March 17, 2010. Available online at http://www.mediawatchwatch.org.uk/2010/03/17/saudi-lawyer-uses-uk-libel-to-sue-danish-papers/

282 "Free Speech is under assault," The Arizona Republic, March 2, 2010. Available online at http://www.azcentral.com/arizonarepublic/opinions/articles/2010/03/02/20100302tue1-02.html

283 "Denmark wants Brussels to stop UK Mohammed cartoon lawsuit," by Leigh Phillips, EUobserver, March 16, 2010. Available online at http://euobserver.com/22/29696

284 On February 22, 2010, the Arizona Senate unanimously passed SB 1268, which is substantively identical to the anti-libel tourism law previously enacted by the state of New York.

285 http://www.govtrack.us/congress/bill.xpd?bill=h111-2765

for defamation" unless the foreign judgment is in compliance with First Amendment protections.[286]

Similarly, the UK Libel Working Group released its report on March 23, 2010, which considered "whether the law of libel, including the law relating to 'libel tourism', in England and Wales was in need of reform and, if so, to make recommendations as to solutions."[287] The Working Group recommended additional procedures that would make libel tourists demonstrate why the United Kingdom is the proper venue for their complaints,[288] modifying the multiple publication rule,[289] and partially codifying a public interest defense.[290]

As governmental and private sector ripostes to Islamist lawfare continue to develop, journalists should be confident that they may write knowing their essential rights under US law are being protected against emerging legal threats, just as previous generations of journalists have been against the threats of their time.

No book will entirely thaw the chill that has descended upon free speech as the result of Islamist lawfare and political correctness. Success will only be achieved through the actions of journalists, writing free from fear of reprisal and firm in the knowledge that they are exercising their rights in the grand tradition of American history.

---

286 The bill, as passed by both houses of Congress, is available at
http://www.gpo.gov/fdsys/pkg/BILLS-111hr2765enr/pdf/BILLS-111hr2765enr.pdf

287 "Report of the Libel Working Group," Ministry of Justice, March 23, 2010. Available online at
http://www.justice.gov.uk/publications/docs/libel-working-group-report.pdf

288 Id at 16.

289 Id at 21.

290 Id at 33. In the UK, there is a qualified privilege for journalists reporting on matters of public interest. Known as the "Reynolds defense," it comes from the landmark decision in Reynolds v. Times Newspapers Ltd [2001] 2 A.C. 127.

" For speech concerning public affairs is more than self-expression; it is the essence of self-government.

Justice William J. Brennan, Jr.,
Garrison v. Louisiana [291]

---

291 379 U.S. 64, 74-75 (1964)

ABOUT THE AUTHORS

Aaron Eitan Meyer is a researcher and analyst, legal correspondent for the Terror Finance Blog, and is on the advisory board for the digital advocacy group Act for Israel. He has served as research director of The Lawfare Project, director of research for the Children's Rights Institute, and assistant director of the Legal Project at the Middle East Forum. He received his B.A. from New School University, and his J.D. from Touro College Jacob D. Fuchsberg Law Center.

Mr. Meyer's work has appeared in the Terror Finance Blog, Covenant, Washington Post Online, Washington Times, The American Spectator, Counter Terrorist magazine, ILSA Journal of International & Comparative Law, Big Peace, the Legal Project of the Middle East Forum's blog, Islamist Watch, and the Lawfare Project's blog. Mr. Meyer has lectured at Yeshiva University and presented at the annual convention of the Association for the Study of the Middle East and Africa (ASMEA).

Mr. Meyer's current areas of research include lawfare, terror finance, child suicide bombers, and Major General Orde Charles Wingate.

Brooke Goldstein is a New York City based human rights attorney and award-winning filmmaker. She serves as director of The Lawfare Project,[292] a nonprofit organization dedicated to raising awareness about and facilitating a response to the abuse of Western legal systems and human rights law. She is also the founder and director of the Children's Rights Institute (CRI),[293] a not-for-profit organization whose mission is to track, spotlight as well as legally combat violations of children's basic human rights as occurring throughout the globe. CRI has a special focus on the state-sponsored indoctrination and recruitment of children to become suicide-homicide bombers, child soldiers and human shields.

From 2007-2009 Brooke served as director of the Legal Project at the Middle East Forum, an organization that arranges financial support for, and pro-bono legal representation of persons wrongfully sued for exercising their right to free speech on issues of national security and public concern.

Brooke's award-winning documentary film, *The Making of a Martyr* uncovers the illegal, state-sponsored indoctrination and recruitment of Palestinian children for suicide-homicide attacks. Filming *Martyr,* ahe secured first hand interviews with active and armed members of the Al-Aqsa, Fatah, Islamic Jihad and Hamas terrorist groups as well as with families of suicide bombers, children imprisoned for attempting to blow themselves up, teachers at terrorist-run schools and others involved in the phenomenon of child suicide bombing. *Martyr* is currently

---

292 *See* www.TheLawfareProject.org
293 *See* www.ChidrensRightsInstitute.org

broadcast on television stations throughout the globe and was listed as IMDB's eighth most popular title on the West Bank.

She is a regular commentator on FOX News and has been featured in several media including CNN, *The New York Sun, Swindle Magazine*, Defense Technology International and on WABC News Talk Radio and has been published in a variety of sources including the New York *Daily News, The American Spectator*, the Washington *Times, The Counter Terrorist, Special Ops Magazine* as well as others.

Brooke is a seasoned public speaker and has lectured and taught seminars at numerous schools including the Benjamin N. Cardozo School of Law, New York University, Berkeley University, and Stanford University, amongst others. Brooke has also been invited to brief government officials at the U.S. State Department, the White House, the Pentagon, the U.K. Parliament, and U.S. Central Command on issues of asymmetric warfare and human rights.

She is the 2007 recipient of the E. Nathaniel Gates Award for Outstanding Public Advocacy, the 2009 Inspire! Award bestowed by the Benjamin N Cardozo School of Law, was listed in 2009 as one of '36 Under 36 Young Innovators' by the Jewish Week, formerly served as an adjunct fellow at the Hudson Institute, is currently an associate fellow at the Henry Jackson Society and a Lincoln Fellow at the Claremont Institute.

Additionally, she is the co-founder of A2B Film Productions, Inc., a Canadian-based independent documentary film production company focused on creating films that explore issues ignored by the mainstream media.

Canadian born, Brooke earned her B.A. from McGill University and received her J.D. from the Benjamin N. Cardozo

School of Law. She also attended Columbia University and University of Toronto.

APPENDIX A: ARTICLES ON
ISLAMIST LAWFARE

The primary focus of this book is to inform journalists and others who write about controversial topics in this age of lawfare, about their free speech rights under U.S. law. Attempts by collective entities and individuals to silence free speech about Islam, terrorism and their funding encompasses a complicated topic that cannot be adequately set forth in this book. Three illustrative examples of analysis are appended for those interested in the phenomenon. The first such article is broad in scope and serves as a general introduction to Islamist lawfare with a number of case examples both publicly known and underreported. The second article was written following the death of Khalid bin Mahfouz, known as the "Libel Tourist," and cautions against allowing a tactical manifestation of lawfare to detract from a comprehensive strategic response. The third and final article was written in response to complaints filed with Canadian Human Rights Commissions against author Mark Steyn, and represents one of the first analyses of Islamist lawfare as more than a series of isolated cases.

HOW ISLAMIST LAWFARE TACTICS TARGET FREE SPEECH[294]

Brooke Goldstein and Aaron Eitan Meyer

The Counter Terrorist, April 29, 2009

Are American authors who write about terrorism and its sources of financing safe? Are counter-terrorist advisors to the New York City Police department safe? Are U.S. congressmen safe when they report terrorist front groups to the FBI and CIA? Are cartoonists who parody Mohammad safe from arrest?

Must a Dutch politician who produced a documentary film quoting the Koran stand trial for blasphemy of Islam in Jordan? Is anyone who speaks publicly on the threat of militant Islam safe from frivolous and malicious lawsuits designed to bankrupt, punish, and silence them? These days, the answer is no.

Lawfare is usually defined as the use of the law as a weapon of war,[295] or the pursuit of strategic aims through aggressive legal maneuvers.[296] Traditionally, lawfare tactics have been used to obtain moral advantages over the enemy in the court of public opinion,[297] and to intimidate heads of state from acting out of fear of prosecution for war crimes.[298] Al-Qaeda training manuals

---

294 The article originally appeared in two parts in The Counter Terrorist magazine, February/March and April/May 2009.To see these in PDF form: Part 1 and 2. Online at http://www.centerforsecuritypolicy.org/p18029.xml?cat_id=313

295 Dunlap, Law and Military Interventions: Preserving Humanitarian Values in 21st Century Conflicts (29 Nov 2001), and David Rivkin, The Wall Street Journal Op Ed at http://online.wsj.com/article/SB117220137149816987.html (commentary at: http://www.prospect.org/cs/articles?article=the_lawfare_scare)

296 http://www.opinionjournal.com/forms/printThis.html?id=110005366

297 http://online.wsj.com/article/SB117220137149816987.html

298 Israeli Minister Avi Dichter canceled a trip to Britain after being threatened with arrest over a 2002 incident, (See http://www.timesonline.co.uk/tol/news/uk/article3012503.ece) Also, Israeli Deputy Prime Minister and former Israel Defense Forces Chief of Staff Shaul Mofaz cut short a trip to Britain after "the director of public prosecutions in England asked police in London to investigate

instruct its captured militants to file claims of torture or other forms of abuse so as to reposition themselves as victims against their captors.[299] The 2004 decision by the United Nation's International Court of Justice declaring Israel's security fence a crime against humanity, which pointedly ignored the fact that the fence contributed to a sharp decline in terror attacks, is another example of lawfare aimed at public opinion.[300]

Yet, lawfare has moved beyond gaining mere moral advantages over nation-states and winning lawsuits against government actors. Over the past ten years, we have seen a steady increase in lawfare tactics directly targeting the human rights of North American and European civilians in order to constrain the free flow of public information about militant Islam.

THE ISLAMIST MOVEMENT

The Islamist movement is that which seeks to impose tenets of Islam, and specifically Shari'a law, as a legal, political, religious, and judicial authority both in Muslim states and in the West. It is generally composed of two wings-that which operates violently, propagating suicide-homicide bombing and other terrorist activities; and that which operates lawfully, conducting a "soft jihad" within our media, government, and court systems; through Shari'a banking;[301] and within our school systems.[302]

---

war crimes allegations." (See

http://www.smh.com.au/articles/2002/11/01/1036027036796.html)

299 "Lawfare" By David B. Rivkin & Lee A. Casey, The Wall Street Journal (Feb 26, 2007) at http://prasad.aem.cornell.edu/doc/media/PrasadRajan.WSJAFeb07.pdf

300 For the text of the decision see: http://www.icj-cij.org/docket/index.php?p1=3&p2=4&k=5a&case=131&code=mwp&p3=4

301 For more information on Shari'a compliant financing see David Yerushalmi, "Sharia's Black Box: Civil Liability and Criminal Exposure Surrounding Sharia-Compliant Finance," Utah Law Review or www.securefreedom.org

302 Much has been said about the Saudi effort to produce school textbooks for American grade schools, and the establishment of Islamic-language public schools such as the Khalil Gibran

Yet Islamism, the drive to promulgate Islamic values as they are defined by various Imams and Muslim leaders, is the ideology that powers not only Hamas and Al-Qaeda, but motivates organizations such as the Canadian Islamic Congress, the Islamic Circle of North America, and the Council on American Islamic Relations.[303]

Both the violent and the lawful arms of the Islamist movement can and do work apart, but often, their work reinforces each other's. For example, one tenet of Shari'a law is to punish those who criticize Islam and to silence speech considered blasphemous of its prophet Mohammad. While the violent arm of the Islamist movement attempts to silence speech by burning cars when Danish cartoons of Mohammed are published, by

---

Academy in New York, raising issues of Establishment Clause violations and contravening separation of church and state, or more accurately, Mosque and state. "Islam in America's public schools: Education or indoctrination?" http://www.sfgate.com/cgi-bin/article.cgi?f=/g/a/2008/06/11/cstillwell.DTL On New York's "Khalil Gibran International Academy" http://www.danielpipes.org/blog/2007/03/on-new-yorkskhalil-gibran-international.html

303 CAIR: "CAIR believes the active practice of Islam strengthens the social and religious fabric of our nation." http://www.cair.com/AboutUs/VisionMissionCorePrinciples.aspx. CAIR also offers a 'guide' which offers "...background information about Islam and Muslims, best practices on reporting on the Muslim community and a list of accurate terminology to use when covering issues relating to Islam." Also, they have a campaign to 'Explore the Quran' with the following description of their aim: "In today's climate of heightened religious sensitivities and apparent cultural clashes, now is the time for people of all faiths to better acquaint themselves with Islam's sacred text, the Holy Quran." http://www.explorethequran.org This is to be accomplished by distributing copies of the Quran. There is a similar campaign regarding Muhammad. http://www.exploremuhammad.org ISNA: Imam Sirraj Wahhaj, listed as Member, ISNA Majlis Ashura: "In time, this so-called democracy will crumble, and there will be nothing. And the only thing that will remain will be Islam," Wahhaj was quoted as saying in one of his sermons. as cited in "Radical Imam Promotes Pro-Islamic Ad Campaign to Run on New York Subways" http://www.foxnews.com/story/0,2933,387701,00.html CAIR: Omar M. Ahmad, then-director of CAIR: "If you choose to live here (in America) ... you have a responsibility to deliver the message of Islam..." in "American Muslim leader urges faithful to spread Islam's message" and "The Koran, the Muslim book of scripture, should be the highest authority in America, and Islam the only accepted religion on earth..." Article by Lisa Gardiner Available online at http://www.danielpipes.org/394.pdf See also, The WorldNetDaily "Did CAIR founder say Islam to Rule America?" http://www.worldnetdaily.com/news/article.asp?ARTICLE_ID=53303

murdering film directors such as Theo Van Gogh, and by forcing thinkers such as Wafa Sultan into hiding out of fear for her life, the lawful arm is skillfully maneuvering within Western court systems, hiring lawyers and suing to silence its critics.

LEGAL JIHAD

Islamist states, organizations, and individuals with financial means have launched a "legal jihad," filing a series of malicious lawsuits in American courts and abroad, designed to punish and silence those who engage in public discourse about militant Islam. Such lawsuits are being used as a weapon of war against counter-terrorism experts, law enforcement personnel, politicians, and anyone working to disseminate information on Islamist terrorism and its sources of financing. The lawsuits are often predatory, filed without a serious expectation of winning, and undertaken as a means to intimidate, demoralize, and bankrupt defendants. Claims are often based on frivolous charges ranging from defamation to workplace harassment, from "hate speech" to "Islamophobia," and have resulted in books being banned and pulped, thousands of dollars worth of fines, and publishing houses and newspapers rejecting important works on counter-terrorism out of fear of being the next target.

By suing to impose penalties and gag orders on counter-terrorism experts, government officials, authors, and the media, noncombatants who engage in Islamist lawfare are assuming critical support roles, whether intentionally or not, for violent operations that seek to establish principles of Shari'a law in the West. The following cases represent a small percentage of Islamist lawfare in the U.S., but are illustrative.

In 2003, the Washington-based Council on American Islamic Relations (CAIR), sued former U.S. Congressman Cass

Ballenger after an interview with the congressman revealed that he had reported the group to the CIA and FBI as a "fundraising arm for Hezbollah."[304] Fortunately, the judge in Ballenger's case ruled the congressman's statements were made in the scope of his public duties and were therefore constitutionally protected speech in the interest of public concern.

The following year, CAIR instituted a 1.3 million dollar lawsuit against Andrew Whitehead, an American activist and blogger, for maintaining the website Anti-CAIR-net.org, on which CAIR is described as an Islamist organization with ties to terrorist groups. After refusing Whitehead's discovery requests, seemingly afraid of what internal documents the legal process it had initiated would reveal, CAIR withdrew its claims against Whitehead, a settlement was reached, and the case was dismissed by the court with prejudice.[305]

In 2005, the Islamic Society of Boston (ISB) filed a lawsuit charging defamation against a dozen defendants including the Boston Herald, FOX 25 News, counterterrorism expert Steven Emerson, and several others. The defendants were targeted by ISB for publicly speaking about the Islamic Society's connections to militant Islam and for raising questions about the construction of its Saudi-funded mosque in Boston. A full two years after it had initiated the lawsuit, and just a few months after the discovery process was initiated into ISB's financial records, ISB dropped its

---

304 Ballenger made the comment in a phone conversation to journalist Tim Funk of the Charlotte Observer on October 1, 2003. As cited by the Court in Council of American Islamic Relations, v. Cass Ballenger, 444 F.3d 659 (D.C. Cir. 2006)
http://pacer.cadc.uscourts.gov/docs/common/opinions/200604/05-5161a.pdf
305 Despite CAIR's failed effort at intimidation, Whitehead's Anti-CAIR website is still up and running along with the text that was at issue and is available at www.anti-cairnet.org

case and abandoned all of its claims against all of the defendants, without receiving any form of payment.[306]

Bruce Tefft, a former CIA official and counter-terrorism consultant for the NYPD, was sued by a Muslim police officer for "workplace harassment" after Tefft sent out emails to a voluntary recipient list of police officers containing information about militant Islamic terrorism.[307] Tefft's suit is ongoing. Sometimes American authors and publishers wrongfully targeted are able to take advantage of Anti-SLAPP statutes, the acronym being Anti-Strategic Litigation Against Public Participation. Anti-SLAPP statutes have been enacted in several, but not all, U.S. states and are aimed at preventing lawsuits designed to hinder legitimate public dialogue. The problem, however, with Anti-SLAPP statutes is threefold-not all states have enacted them, there is no federal equivalent, and one must wait to be sued in order to take advantage of them.

Such was the case when American author Matthew Levitt and his publisher, Yale Press, were sued by KinderUSA for Levitt's book Hamas, in which Levitt describes KinderUSA as a charitable front for terror financing. In response to the lawsuit, Levitt and Yale Press instituted a counter-claim based on California's Anti-SLAPP statute arguing that KinderUSA's suit was a disguised attempt at wrongfully intimidating them into silence. Shortly after

---

306 In line with the old adage that actions speak louder than words, the fact that both ISB and CAIR abandoned their claims right before they would have been required, by court order, to turn over internal documents speaks volumes about whether the two plaintiffs had ever intended to pursue their legal claims on their merit or had instead, intended to use the court system to intimidate the defendants as well as other journalists, into not reporting on their activities.

307 http://frontpagemagazine.com/Articles/Read.aspx?GUID=AF613BFA-8E34-4A07-8DB4-20D89DE3D84B

the counter-claim was filed, KinderUSA mysteriously dropped its lawsuit, claiming only that it found the suit too costly to pursue.[308]

Most disturbing, however, are the examples of parties sued for reporting on official U.S. government investigations into terrorist activities, or for formally appealing to government authorities to conduct investigations into suspected illegal activity. Parties targeted in this vein include the New York Times, which, in 2001, reported on the U.S. government's investigation of the Global Relief Foundation and was subsequently sued;[309] The Wall Street Journal, which, in 2002, reported on the monitoring of Saudi bank accounts and was also sued;[310] and the Anti-Defamation League, which, in 2002, called for the investigation of a public school superintendent named Khadija Ghafur, based on indications that schools under his supervision were teaching religion in violation of the establishment clause. Ghafur predictably sued ADL for libel and lost, but only after much time and money was spent by ADL defending itself.[311]

The cumulative effect of these lawsuits, combined with the looming threat of future lawsuits, is creating a detrimental chilling effect on the exercise of free speech within this country, and raising the cost of public debate about the war on terrorism. Islamist lawfare has also sparked a wave of self-censorship, with publishing houses going as far as hiring security experts to assess

---

308 KinderUSA claimed that its resources were better spent on charity.
http://www.libraryjournal.com/info/CA6470780.html

309 In affirming the decision, the 7th Circuit Court of Appeals reiterated that "Truth is an absolute bar to recovery for defamation." 390 F.3d 973 (7th Cir. 2004) http://cases.justia.com/us-court-of-appeals/F3/390/973/506579/

310 The bank dropped the suit in 2005, but the WSJ published a 'clarification' that it had not in fact reported any allegation that linked the bank to terrorism.
http://online.wsj.com/article/SB118530038250476405.html

311 "Court throws out Muslim educator's suit against ADL" http://www.jewishsf.com/content/2-0-/module/displaystory/story_id/20626/edition_id/422/format/html/displaystory.html

the potential for violent reactions in the Muslim community to printed words.

The strategy of silencing Western material "blasphemous" of Islam began not with objections to truth, cartoons, politicians, or political articles. After the 1988 publication of Salman Rushdie's famous work of fiction, The Satanic Verses, Iran's Ayatollah Khomeini issued his infamous fatwa against Rushdie, a British citizen at the time.[312] The fatwa marked the beginning of the end of open discourse-fictional or otherwise-on Islam. Only six months ago, the deputy head of the Khomeini Archives proudly stated on Iranian television that "Imam Khomeini's fatwa on Salman Rushdie has historic significance for Islam. It was not just a fatwa; it was a verdict that still holds today."[313] From this epochal attack, Islamists have moved on to silencing public discourse on issues of national security directly, even as they still seek to quash creative works of fiction to which they object. Though Salman Rushdie published The Satanic Verses in 1988, he remains in hiding a full 20 years later.

Most recently, Random House Publishing Group pulled a fictional novel, The Jewel of Medina, by journalist Sherry Jones about the Prophet Mohammad's child bride. The publishing house feared it would prove offensive to some in the Muslim community and "incite acts of violence."[314] Prior to making its decision public, Thomas Perry, deputy publisher at Random House, consulted with security experts and scholars on Islam and

---

312 For an excellent synopsis and explanation of these events, see "The Ayatollah, the Novelist, and the West" by Daniel Pipes, available online at http://www.danielpipes.org/article/186

313 http://www.danielpipes.org/blog/2004/06/is-salman-rushdie-now-safe.html

314 "Random House Pulls Novel on Islam, Fears Violent," by Edith Honan, (Aug 7, 2008) at: http://www.reuters.com/article/newsOne/idUSN0736008820080807

received "from credible and unrelated sources"[315] cautionary advice not to publish the work.

Denise Spellberg, an associate professor of Islamic history at the University of Texas, made what was described as a "frantic" appeal to drop a "very ugly, stupid piece of work," that she said "made fun of Muslims and their history." [316]Despite the commercial success of fictional pieces about the war on militant Islam, such as the *New York Times'* bestseller *The Last Patriot*,[317] written by Brad Thor and published by Atria Books, and Daniel Silva's *Secret Servant*, published by Putnam, Random House seems to be leaving its business decisions up to articulate professors of Islamic studies. Although the publication of the book was officially postponed for "safety reasons," it is certainly open to question whether the hysterical response of an associate professor constitutes a credible danger. Chastising Random House further, the Islamic Community in Serbia released a statement claiming it was not satisfied with the mere withdrawal of the novel and the organization's leader, Muamer Zukorlic, demanded all of the published copies be handed in.[318]

The cases listed above reflect a few of the same battles going on now: Free speech of Americans and other Westerners being placed under siege by Islamists. Those targeted run the range from government officials actively engaged in battling Islamist terrorism to novelists who dare to use Islamic themes or history in their writing. What must be appreciated, is the fact that this problem is

---

315 http://www.telegraph.co.uk/news/uknews/2524540/Random-Housescraps-publication-of-novel-on-Prophet-Mohammeds-child-bride.html

316 http://dick-meom.blogspot.com/2008/08/random-house-randomlydecides-not-to.html

317 The book is available at: amazon.com: http://www.amazon.com/Last-Patriot-Thriller-Brad-Thor/dp/141654383X/ref=pd_bbs_sr_1?ie=UTF8&s=books&qid=1218036222&sr=8-1

318 http://domino.un.org/UNISPAL.NSF

by no means limited to lawsuits within the United States, or even lawsuits involving U.S. citizens. As lawfare continues to be increasingly utilized the world over, the stakes for Western democracies, including the United States, continue to be raised significantly.

LAWFARE IN EUROPE AND CANADA

Islamist lawfare is achieving a high degree of success in Canada and Europe because their judicial systems and laws do not afford their citizens, or American citizens for that matter, the level of free speech protection granted under the U.S. Constitution. With their "hate speech" legislation, liberal libel laws and virtual codification of "Islamophobia" as a cause of action, European and Canadian legislatures have laid down what could be called the ideal framework for litigious Islamists to achieve their goals.

In February of 2006, the European Union and former UN Secretary General Kofi Annan issued a joint statement with the Organization of the Islamic Conference, in which they recognized the need "to show sensitivity" in treating issues of special significance for the adherents of any particular religion, "even by those who do not share the belief in question."[319] In June of 2006, the Council of Europe hosted a "Programme of the Hearing on European Muslim Communities confronted with Extremism," for which a 'Point of View on the Situation of Europe' was presented by none other than Tariq Ramadan.[320] Based on a draft resolution and the proceedings of June 2006, the Council of Europe recently

---

319
http://domino.un.org/UNISPAL.NSF/fd807e46661e3689852570d00069e918/48c61023cd1909
6f8525710e006df80b!OpenDocument
320
http://assembly.coe.int/Main.asp?link=/Documents/WorkingDocs/Doc08/EDOC11540.htm

released Resolution 1605, asserting widespread 'Islamophobia' and calling all member nations to "condemn and combat Islamophobia."[321]

Persons held accountable to the EU's new legal standards include actress Brigitte Bardot, who was charged this past April, for the fifth time, with "inciting racial hatred" against Muslims and forced to pay a fine of twelve thousand pounds.[322] At the time of her death in 2006, noted Italian author Orianna Fallaci was being sued in France,[323] Italy,[324] Switzerland[325] and other jurisdictions by groups dedicated to preventing the dissemination of her work.

On May 13, 2008, Dutch police actually arrested a cartoonist using the pseudonym Gregorious Nekschot, "...for the criminal offense of "publishing cartoons which are discriminating for Muslims and people with dark skin."[326]

ENGLAND

UK courts, because of their libel laws, are particularly friendly jurisdictions for Islamists who want to restrict the dissemination of material drawing attention to militant Islam and terror financing.[327]

---

321 Adopted by the Council of Europe Parliamentary Assembly, April 15, 2008
http://assembly.coe.int/Main.asp?link=/Documents/AdoptedText/ta08/ERES1605.htm

322 http://www.reuters.com/article/entertainmentNews/idUSL1584799120080415?feedT;
http://www.dailymail.co.uk/tvshowbiz/article-1023969/Brigitte-Bardot-fined-12-000-racial-hatred-claiming-Muslims-destroying-France.html

323 http://www.secularism.org.uk/39371.html#oriana

324 http://www.cbc.ca/story/arts/national/2006/09/15/orianafallaci-obit.html

325 http://www.milligazette.com/Archives/01072002/0107200263.htm

326 http://www.brusselsjournal.com/node/3257

327 Where, in the United States, with our First Amendment rights to free speech, libel plaintiffs not only have the burden to prove that the speech in question is false and defamatory, but where matters of public concern are at issue, the libel plaintiff must also show that the speech was published with a reckless disregard for the truth. In England, on the other hand, the burden is in exactly the opposite direction: the offending speech is presumed to be false, and it is up to the defendant to prove that it is in fact true. While on the surface the difference may seem trite, UK libel jurisprudence, in direct

A major player on this front is Khalid bin Mahfouz, a wealthy businessman who resides in Saudi Arabia and who has been accused by several parties of financially supporting Al Qaeda. A notable libel tourist, Mahfouz has sued or threatened to sue more than 30 publishers and authors in British courts, including several Americans, whose written works have linked him to terrorist entities. Faced with the prospect of protracted and expensive litigation, most of the parties targeted by Mahfouz have issued apologies and retractions, while some have also paid fines and "contributions" to his charities.

In 2007, when Mahfouz threatened to sue Cambridge University Press for publishing the book *Alms for Jihad*, by American authors Robert Collins and J Millard Burr, Cambridge Press immediately capitulated, offered a public apology to Mahfouz, took the book out of print, destroyed the unsold copies of the book, and made the outrageous demand that libraries all over the world remove the book from their shelves.

Shortly after the US publication of Rachel Ehrenfeld's book *Funding Evil*, Mahfouz sued Ehrenfeld for defamation because she too had written about financial ties between Mahfouz and terrorist entities. The allegations against Ehrenfeld were heard by the UK court despite the fact that neither Mahfouz nor Ehrenfeld resides in England, while and the court asserted jurisdiction over her merely because approximately 23 copies of *Funding Evil* were sold to UK buyers online via Amazon.com. Unwilling to travel to England or acknowledge the authority of

---

contrast to US law and due process considerations, effectively operates to declare defendants guilty before proven innocent and UK courts have become a magnet for libel suits that would otherwise fail miserably in the US. And so heavy is the burden of proof put on the defendant that the mere threat of suit in a UK court is enough to intimidate publishers into silence, regardless of the merit of their author's works.

English libel laws over herself and her work, Ehrenfeld lost on default and was ordered to pay heavy fines, apologize, and destroy her books—all of which she refused to do.[328]

Canada, with its "human rights" commissions, joins the list of countries whose laws are being used to attack the free speech rights of authors and activists. Section 13 of the Canadian Human Rights Act bans the electronic transmission of material that is deemed "likely to expose persons to hatred or contempt by reason of the fact that those persons are identifiable on the basis of a prohibited ground of discrimination,"[329] which prohibited grounds include both ethnic origin and religion.[330] Such vagaries in what was probably a well-meaning, yet democratically incompatible and short-sighted law, has enabled a wave of "human rights" complaints in the Canadian Human Rights Commissions (CHRC) against outspoken critics of militant Islam and their publishers.

---

328 Instead, Ehrenfeld went on the offensive and counter-sued Mahfouz in a New York State court seeking to have the foreign judgment declared unenforceable in the United States. Ironically, Ehrenfeld lost her case against Mahfouz, because the New York court decided it lacked jurisdiction over the Saudi resident who, the court said, did not have sufficient connections to the state. Shortly afterwards and in direct response to the court's ruling, the NY state legislature, in an unprecedented show of cross party solidarity, unanimously voted to enact the Libel Terrorism Protection Act which prevents the enforcement of foreign libel judgments over American authors and provides the opportunity for the claim to be tried in the US, on its merits, and according to American principles of free speech. A similar piece of legislation has been introduced in Congress by Arlen Specter and Joseph Lieberman in the Senate and by Joseph King in the House of Representatives, along with several co-sponsors.

329 What is particularly disturbing about Section 13 "hate speech" laws is that the court costs of any one plaintiff who files a section 13 complaint are entirely subsidized by the government, while the defendants are left to endure the financial burden of litigation alone. This is a rule that, on its face, obviously encourages frivolous litigation. Moreover the CHRC has had a one hundred percent conviction rate on section 13 charges.

330 As defined by Section 3 (1) of the Canadian Human Rights Act

The CHRC—as well as local Human Rights Commissions in Ontario, British Columbia, and Alberta—have received complaints along these lines. These have included *Maclean's* magazine, award-winning author Mark Steyn, and noted Canadian lawyer and blogger Ezra Levant. The complaints against *Maclean's* and Steyn were initiated by the Canadian Islamic Congress (CIC) and based on *Maclean's'* re-publication of excerpts from Steyn's book *America Alone*, which details Europe's capitulation to militant Islam, and projects America as potentially the last bastion of freedom, and which the CIC[331] argued in its complaint is "flagrantly Islamophobic."

Levant was likewise hauled before the Commissions on charges of "hate speech" against Muslims after re-publishing the Danish Cartoon of Mohammad in the now-defunct *Western Standard Magazine*. Though the charges against him were dropped the outcome could hardly be considered a "win" for free speech, as he details on his website.[332]

THE NETHERLANDS

The most frightening predicament of all is that of Dutch politician, filmmaker and outspoken critic of militant Islam, Geert Wilders. After releasing a ten-minute self-produced film "Fitna," Wilders has found himself wound up in a litany of "hate speech" litigation, one such suit filed by a radical Imam asking for fifty five thousand Euros in compensation for his hurt feelings. Ironically, the film's narrative is primarily comprised of quotes from the

---

331 The CIC, whose president Mohamed Elmasry once labeled every adult Jew in Israel a legitimate target for terrorists, has previously tried, albeit unsuccessfully, to sue publications it disagrees with in regular Canadian courts of law, including the National Post.

332 http://ezralevant.com/2008/08/punished-first-acquitted-later.html

Koran and scenes of an Imam preaching death to Jews.[333] Most disturbing however, is the fact that the State of Jordan, most likely acting as a stalking house for the Organization of the Islamic Conference (OIC), has issued a request for Wilders' extradition to stand in Jordan for blasphemy, a crime for which Shari'a law declares the penalty to be death, though reports have emerged claiming that the maximum potential sentence would be three years.[334]

The Dutch parliament is taking the request very seriously, and has shut out Wilders from any multi-lateral negotiations. As a precaution, Wilders no longer travels abroad unless he can obtain a diplomatic letter from the destination state promising he won't be extradited. At present, Wilders lives under looming death threats complemented by the threat that any day, Interpol may issue a warrant for his arrest at Jordan's behest.

If Jordan succeeds in extraditing a democratically elected official to stand trial in a non-democratic country for speech made in the scope of his duties while educating his constituents vis-à-vis their national security, all under the guise of blasphemy of Islam, what kind of precedent would be set? As much as the Islamists wish to punish Wilders, there is no question that his case is a dry run for bigger game. How long until some convenient court in an OIC nation decides to find another government official guilty of 'blasphemy' and demands their extradition?

After Italian Minister Roberto Calderoli publicly wore a T-shirt depicting Mohammad, he was forced to resign.[335] Upon his re-nomination to Prime Minister Berlusconi's reformed

---

333 Fitna is available for viewing here: http://video.google.com/videoplay?docid=-2949546475561399959&hl=en

334 http://jihadwatch.org/archives/2008/07/021595print.html

335 http://news.bbc.co.uk/2/hi/europe/4727606.stm

government, thinly veiled threats of "catastrophic consequences" emerging from Libya forced Calderoli to issue a full public apology for his wardrobe.[336]

THE INTERNATIONAL SCENE: MUSLIM
ORGANIZATIONS AND THE UN

National lawfare efforts are being complemented with similar International efforts to outlaw blasphemy of Islam as a crime against humanity. Islamist organizations such as the Muslim World League are calling for the establishment of an independent commission to take action against parties who defame their Prophet Mohammed,[337] and at the Dakar summit, taking legal action against parties who slander Islam was a key issue debated at length, with the final communiqué adopted by the Organization of the Islamic Conference denouncing the "rise in intolerance and discrimination against Muslim minorities, which constitute(s) and affront to human dignity."[338] The Islamic Conference of Foreign Ministers at its thirty-fourth session in Islamabad, in May 2007, condemned the "growing trend of Islamophobia"[339] and emphasized "the need to take effective measures to combat defamation." The Islamic Society of North America and the Muslim Public Affairs Council have both stated publicly that they are considering filing defamation lawsuits against their critics[340] and CAIR has announced an ambitious fundraising goal of one

---

336 http://thestar.com.my/news/story.asp?file=/2008/5/10/worldupdates/2008-05-10T052806Z_01_NOOTR_RTRMDNC_0_-335051-2&sec=Worldupdates

337 http://www.arabnews.com/?page=4&section=0&article=77639&d=28&m=12&y=2006

338 Final Communiqué adopted by the Organization of the Islamic Conference at its eleventh summit in Dakar (March 2008) OIC/SUMMIT-11/2008/FC/Final http://www.oic-oci.org/oicnew/is11/English/FC-11-%20SUMMIT-en.pdf

339 UN HRC Res. 7/19

340 http://www.faithfreedom.org/oped/RobertKing50905.htm and http://www.frontpagemag.com/Articles/Printable.aspx?GUID={1E2DE909-C6F5-4A5F-B852-0D90BE4FEA9C}

million, in part to; "defend against defamatory attacks on Muslims and Islam."[341]

Most recently, Muslim states and organizations have successfully lobbied the United Nations' Human Rights Commission to enact Resolution 7/19,[342] a document that turns the concept of "human rights" into an instrument of Orwellian thought control. The Resolution makes reference to the Durban Declaration, and expresses the intent "to complement legal strategies" aimed at criminalizing the defamation of religion. The Resolution "urges States to provide, within their respective legal and constitutional systems, adequate protections against acts of... discrimination,"[343] and prohibits "the dissemination of racist and xenophobic ideas."[344] Note that it is ideas that are prevented here, not published words but defamatory thoughts against Islam which the United Nations is banning.

The Resolution further expresses its "deep concern at the attempts to identify Islam with terrorism, violence and human rights violations." What are the chances that this provision will be applied to those who behead journalists in the name of Islam, or to Palestinian terrorist groups that call themselves 'Islamic Jihad'?

To add insult to injury, signatories to the Resolution take the opportunity to "emphasize (emphasis not added) that everyone has the right to freedom of expression" but that this freedom may "be subject to certain restrictions" while stipulating that "the prohibition of the dissemination of ideas (emphasis added) based on racial superiority or hatred is compatible with the

341 http://www.nysun.com/national/treasury-department-tars-alamoudi-founder-of/24211/
342 For the full text of Un HRC Res. 7/19 see
http://ap.ohchr.org/documents/E/HRC/resolutions/A_HRC_RES_7_19.pdf
343 UN HRC Res. 7/19 Section 9
344 49 UN HRC Res. 7/19 Section 9

freedom of opinion and expression." Signatories to UN HRC Res. 7/19 include China, Egypt, Indonesia, Jordan, Malaysia, Nigeria, Pakistan, Philippines, Qatar, the Russian Federation, Saudi Arabia and Sri Lanka, amongst others.

This Resolution 7/19 looks like an initial attempt to establish a body of international law to be used in the future against heads of state who speak out against militant Islam as a threat to national security. Hence, instead of Muslim states unilaterally seeking the extradition of a Geert Wilders—or, perhaps, a Donald Rumsfeld—Islamists can now employ UN mechanisms to force politicians to abide by a standard of 'sensitivity' to Islam defined solely by Islamists themselves.

The European Center for Law and Justice, a not for profit public interest law firm submitted an engaging report to the UN High Commissioner arguing, correctly, that freedom of religion does not entail carte blanche freedom to practice your religion absent criticism. In fact, Resolution 7/19 is itself a violation of international law undermining the inalienable human right to free speech, especially on matters of important public concern such as religion and national security.[345]

Yet what are the positions of the American Civil Liberties Union and the Center for Constitutional Rights (CCR) on this issue? Where is the international media? Why is this issue being met with virtual silence on their behalves while American citizens' basic human rights to free speech are being trampled on? Perhaps the CCR is too busy with its suit against former Defense Secretary Donald Rumsfeld in Spain for alleged "war crimes" in Iraq, since the German case against him was dismissed.[346]

---

345 UN HRC Res. 7/19 Section 8
346 ECLJ report can be found at: http://www.meforum.org/legal-project.php

The war against Islamism is as much a war of ideas as it is a physical battle, and therefore the dissemination of information in the free world is paramount. The manipulation of Western court systems, the use of western "hate speech laws" and other products of political correctness to destroy the very principles that democracies stand for, must be countered.

Unfortunately Islamist lawfare is beginning to limit and control public discussion of Islam, particularly as it pertains to comprehending the threat posed by Islamic terrorist entities. As such, the Islamist lawfare challenge presents a direct and real threat not only to our constitutional rights, but also to our national security.

Some have argued that the anti-Americanism of militant Islamists has little to do with anti-imperialism but reflects a profound contempt for the liberal social democratic society we have built and its emphasis on individual liberties and freedoms.[347] Freedom of expression is the cornerstone of democratic liberty; it is a freedom that Western civilizations have over time paid for with blood. We must not give it up so easily. The true imperialists are those who seek to impose their perception on others, through violent or legal means, and who seek to conquer and subjugate contradictory points of view.

The reality is that the Muslim community has nothing to gain from supporting the censorship of debate about Islam. If a cartoon with Mohammad is "hate speech" now, how much longer before the Koran gets the same treatment? As Jonathan Kay, *National Post* columnist, has aptly pointed out "human rights

---

347 http://jurist.law.pitt.edu/paperchase/2007/04/german-prosecutor-rejects-war-crimes.php

mandarins haven't gone after mosques or mullahs—yet,"[348] but it doesn't take much to recognize that two can play at the same game. The actions of CAIR and the OIC and others who engage in Islamist lawfare offer a great rebuttal to those who see Islamism as compatible with democracy.

---

348 Tarek Fatah, "Triggering a State of Islam," The National Post, May 13, 2008.

ISLAMIST LAWFARE[349]

Aaron Eitan Meyer

The American Spectator, September 15, 2009

On Tuesday, August 18, the Saudi Arabia-based Arab News reported[350] that Khalid bin Mahfouz, the Saudi billionaire perhaps best known in the West as the "Libel Tourist" for his penchant for using U.K. connections to bring libel lawsuits against his critics had passed away.

However, the much-publicized phenomenon of 'libel tourism'—that is, the practice of non-United Kingdom residents suing American researchers and authors for libel in the plaintiff-friendly U.K.—had already effectively met its own demise over a year ago, after Rachel Ehrenfeld's refusal[351] to comply with a British court's default judgment in favor of bin Mahfouz against her led to the enactment of protective legislation in several U.S. states, and consideration of similar bills in Congress.[352]

In fact, bin Mahfouz's only newsworthy success came when he sued for libel over the book *Alms for Jihad: Charity and Terrorism in the Islamic World,* whose publisher, Cambridge University Press, capitulated[353] to him, abjectly apologizing

---

349 Available online at http://spectator.org/archives/2009/09/15/islamist-lawfare and http://www.legal-project.org/article/460

350 "Khalid Bin Mahfouz buried," Arab News, August 18, 2009. Available online at http://www.arabnews.com/?page=1&section=0&article=125575&d=18&m=8&y=2009

351 "Protecting Free Speech," by Brett Joshpe, American Spectator, December 18, 2008. Available online at http://spectator.org/archives/2008/12/18/protecting-free-speech

352 "A Shield for Free Speech, but no Sword against Islamist Lawfare, yet," by Aaron Eitan Meyer, Terror Finance Blog, October 6, 2008. Available online at http://www.terrorfinance.org/the_terror_finance_blog/2008/10/a-shield-for-fr.html

353 "Islamist Lawfare," by Jamie Glazov [interview with Brooke Goldstein], FrontPageMagazine.com, May 12, 2008. Available online at http://97.74.65.51/readArticle.aspx?ARTID=30937

publicly and even requesting that libraries pull copies off of shelves—a request that American libraries categorically refused.[354] However, unlike the Ehrenfeld case, bin Mahfouz's suit over *Alms for Jihad*, reprehensible and predatory though it was, was *not* a case of libel tourism, since *Alms for Jihad* was "Printed in the United Kingdom at the University Press, Cambridge."[355]

Yet, despite its brief and extremely limited existence, libel tourism has been allowed for too long to overshadow the real extent of the threat to free and open discourse on militant Islam, terrorism, and its sources of funding—Islamist legal warfare, or "lawfare."

Unlike libel tourism, Islamist lawfare is not a mere tactic, but part of a grand strategy, and one that uses every legal opportunity possible to achieve its goals: including rewriting international human rights norms to comport with Shari'a-based interpretation,[356] attempts to globally criminalize manufactured and unsubstantiated assertions of "Islamophobia" or "defamation" of religion, claims of "hate speech"[357] or "harassment," and promoting self-censorship by American publishers and media. Even as far as predatory libel lawsuits go, there have been many cases brought within the U.S. without the need to resort to British

---

354 "ALA to Libraries: Keep Alms for Jihad, Pulped in the UK," by Andrew Albanese and Jennifer Pinkowski, LibraryJournal.com, August 23, 2007. Available online at http://www.libraryjournal.com/article/CA6471402.html

355 Frontmatter/Prelims, Alms for Jihad. Available online at http://assets.cambridge.org/97805218/57307/frontmatter/9780521857307_frontmatter.htm

356 "The OIC and the Universality of Human Rights," by Aaron Eitan Meyer, Legal Project Blog, January 12, 2009. Available online at http://www.legal-project.org/blog/2009/01/the-oic-and-the-universality-of-human-rights

357 See, "Death to Free Speech in the Netherlands," by Brooke M. Goldstein and Aaron Eitan Meyer, American Spectator, January 22, 2009. Available online at http://spectator.org/archives/2009/01/22/death-to-free-speech-in-the-ne and http://www.legal-project.org/article/154

libel law, leaving bin Mahfouz's "libel tourism" as generally unnecessary.

Even within the United States, fixating on the predatory domestic libel suits that are a mainstay of Islamist lawfare is dangerously myopic. Counterterrorism consultant Bruce Tefft is being sued by a John Doe Muslim police officer not for libel, but for "workplace harassment."[358] Random House's cowardly decision not to publish the novel *The Jewel of Medina*,[359] like Palgrave McMillan's earlier decision to renege on publishing *QURAN: A Reformist Translation*, had nothing to do with threats of libel lawsuits, but everything to do with Islamist pressure.

Despite these and countless other examples, few are even aware of the term Islamist lawfare, much less the extent of its reach. Conducting an online search for the term "Islamist lawfare" on a major search engine will likely result in somewhere between 14,000 and 18,400 hits, while a search for "libel tourism" will net between 189,000 and 213,000 hits. In part, the number of hits for libel tourism is the positive result of excellent analyses of the phenomenon, such as Andrew C. McCarthy's highly informative article, which appeared in the September, 2008 issue of *Commentary* magazine, where he clearly laid out the crucial public interest at stake, as "the need to understand and address financial support systems that invigorate the terror networks targeting Americans for mass murder."[360]

---

358 "Welcome to 'Lawfare' - A New Type of Jihad," by Brooke Goldstein, Family Security Matters, April 14, 2008. Available online at http://www.legal-project.org/article/241

359 "Random House pulls novel on Islam, fears violence," by Edith Honan, Reuters, August 7, 2008. Available online at http://www.reuters.com/article/idUSN0736008820080807

360 "Can Libel Tourism Be Stopped?" by Andrew C. McCarthy, Commentary, September 2008. Abstract available online at http://www.commentarymagazine.com/viewarticle.cfm/can-libel-tourism-be-stopped--12502

The danger does not stem from the fact that a search for libel tourism nets many results, which demonstrates how effective the response to libel tourism has been, but from the fact that the vastly more complex and dangerous issue of Islamist lawfare has yet to be fully addressed in the public arena.

Perhaps bin Mahfouz's demise will provide an end to the dangerous overemphasis that has been placed on libel tourism. Islamist lawfare is a far larger threat that needs to be understood as such. Otherwise, we in the West will find ourselves further outflanked by Islamist entities with immense political and financial resources—and by a certain point, that could prove sufficient for militant Islam's victory.

MARK STEYN IS NOT ALONE[361]

Brooke M. Goldstein

The American Spectator, January 15, 2008

Award-winning author Mark Steyn has been summoned to appear before two Canadian Human Rights Commissions on vague allegations[362] of "subject[ing] Canadian Muslims to hatred and contempt" and being "flagrantly Islamophobic" after *Maclean's* magazine published an excerpt [363] from his book, *America Alone.*

The public inquisition of Steyn has triggered outrage among Canadians and Americans who value free speech, but it should not come as a surprise. Steyn's predicament is just the latest salvo in a campaign of legal actions designed to punish and silence the voices of anyone who speaks out against Islamism, Islamic terrorism, or its sources of financing.

The Canadian Islamic Congress (CIC), which initiated the complaint against Steyn, has previously tried unsuccessfully to sue publications[364] it disagrees with, including Canada's *National Post.* The not-for-profit organization's president, Mohamed Elmasry, once labeled[365] every adult Jew in Israel a legitimate

---

361 Available online at http://spectator.org/archives/2008/01/15/mark-steyn-is-not-alone and http://www.legal-project.org/article/106

362 "Canadian Islamic Congress launches human rights complaints against Maclean's," by Kate Lunau, Maclean's, November 30, 2007. Available online at http://www.macleans.ca/article.jsp?content=20071130_111821_7448

363 "The future belongs to Islam," by Mark Steyn, Maclean's, October 20, 2006. Available online at http://www.macleans.ca/article.jsp?content=20061023_134898_134898&source

364 "Censorship In The Name Of 'Human Rights'," by Ezra Levant, National Post, December 18, 2007. Available online at http://www.nationalpost.com/opinion/story.html?id=175234

365 "Transcript Of Dr. Mohamed Elmasry's Remarks On Michel Coren Show," October 19, 2004. Available online at http://www.montrealmuslimnews.net/transcript.htm

target for terrorists and is in the habit of accusing[366] his opponents of anti-Islamism—a charge that is now apparently an actionable claim in Canada. In 2006, after Elmasry publicly accused a spokesman for the Muslim Canadian Congress of being anti-Islamic, the spokesman reportedly resigned amidst fears[367] for his personal safety.

The Islamist movement has two wings—one violent and one lawful—which operate apart but often reinforce each other. While the violent arm attempts to silence speech by burning cars when cartoons of Mohammed are published, the lawful arm is maneuvering within Western legal systems.

Islamists with financial means have launched a legal jihad, manipulating democratic court systems to suppress freedom of expression, abolish public discourse critical of Islam, and establish principles of Shariah law. The practice, called "lawfare," is often predatory, filed without a serious expectation of winning and undertaken as a means to intimidate and bankrupt defendants.

Forum shopping, whereby plaintiffs bring actions in jurisdictions most likely to rule in their favor, has enabled a wave of "libel tourism" that has resulted in foreign judgments against European and now American authors mandating the destruction of American-authored literary material.

At the time of her death in 2006, noted Italian author Orianna Fallaci was being sued in France, Italy, Switzerland, and other jurisdictions, by groups dedicated to preventing the dissemination of her work. With its "human rights" commissions,

---

366 "MCC questions motives behind demand to ban debate on religion," by Niaz Salimi, Muslim Canadian Congress, February 24, 2006. Available online at http://www.muslimcanadiancongress.org/20060224.html

367 "Anti-War Movement's Strange Allies: Hard Line Islamists," by Terry Glavin, The Tyee, November 22, 2006. Available online at http://thetyee.ca/Views/2006/11/22/Islamists/

Canada joins the list of countries, including France and the United Kingdom, whose laws are being used to attack the free speech rights and due process protections afforded American citizens.

A major player on this front is Khalid bin Mahfouz, a wealthy Egyptian who resides in Saudi Arabia. Mahfouz has sued or threatened to sue more than 30[368] publishers and authors in British courts, including several Americans, whose written works have linked him to terrorist entities. A notable libel tourist, Mahfouz has taken advantage of the UK's plaintiff-friendly libel laws to restrict the dissemination of written material that draws attention to Saudi-funded terrorism.

Faced with the prospect of protracted and expensive litigation, and regardless of the merit of the works, most authors and publishers targeted have issued apologies and retractions, while some have paid fines and "contributions" to Mahfouz's charities. When Mahfouz threatened Cambridge Press with a lawsuit for publishing *Alms for Jihad* by American authors Robert Collins and J. Millard Burr, the publisher immediately capitulated, offered a public apology to Mahfouz, pulped the unsold copies of the book, and took it out of print.

Shortly after the publication of *Funding Evil* in the United States, Mahfouz sued its author, anti-terrorism analyst and director of the American Center for Democracy, Dr. Rachel Ehrenfeld, for alleging financial ties between wealthy Saudis, including Mahfouz, and terrorist entities such as al Qaeda. The allegations against Ehrenfeld were heard by the UK court despite the fact that neither Mahfouz nor Ehrenfeld resides in England

---

368 "A SLAPP Against Freedom," by Judith Miller, City Journal, Autumn 2007. Available online at http://www.city-journal.org/html/17_4_sndgs01.html

and merely because approximately 23 copies [369]of *Funding Evil* were sold online to UK buyers via Amazon.com.

Unwilling to travel to England or acknowledge the authority of English libel laws over herself and her work, Ehrenfeld lost on default and was ordered to pay heavy fines, apologize, and destroy her books—all of which she has refused to do. Instead, Ehrenfeld counter-sued Mahfouz in a New York State court seeking to have the foreign judgment declared unenforceable in the United States.

Ironically, Ehrenfeld lost her case[370] against Mahfouz, because the New York court ruled it lacked jurisdiction over the Saudi resident who, the court said, did not have sufficient connections to the state. Shortly afterwards the Association of American Publishers released a statement[371] that criticized the ruling as a blow to intellectual freedom and "a deep disappointment for publishers and other First Amendment advocates."

The litany[372] of American publishers, television stations, authors, journalists, experts, activists, political figures, and citizens targeted for censorship is long and merits brief mention. There is an obvious pattern to these suits that can only be ignored at great peril. And we must expect future litigation along these lines:

---

369 "2 international libel cases could benefit U.S. publishers," by Douglas Lee, First Amendment Center, October 18, 2005. Available online at
http://www.firstamendmentcenter.org/analysis.aspx?id=15940

370 "Ehrenfeld Loses in New York Court," by Rebecca Bynum, New English Review, December 23, 2007. Available online at
http://www.newenglishreview.org/blog_display.cfm/blog_id/12009

371 No longer available at
http://www.publishers.org/main/PressCenter/EhrenfeldNYCourtDecision.htm

372 "More Overlooked History: The Muslim Libel Cases," by Jeffrey Breinholt, Counterterrorism Blog, August 2, 2007. Available online at
http://counterterrorismblog.org/2007/08/more_overlooked_history_the_mu.php

- Joe Kaufman, chairman of Americans Against Hate, was served with a temporary restraining order and sued for leading a peaceful and lawful ten person protest against the Islamic Circle of North America (ICNA) outside an event the group sponsored at a Six Flags theme park in Texas. According to ICNA's website, the group is dedicated to "working for the establishment of Islam in all spheres of life," and to "reforming society at large." The complaint included seven Dallas-area plaintiffs who had never been previously mentioned by Kaufman, nor been present at the theme park. Litigation is ongoing.

- The Council on American Islamic Relations (CAIR) sued Andrew Whitehead, an American activist, for $1.3 million for founding and maintaining the website Anti-CAIR-net.org, on which he lists CAIR as an Islamist organization with ties to terrorist groups. After CAIR refused Whitehead's discovery requests, seemingly afraid of what internal documents the legal process it had initiated would reveal, the lawsuit was dismissed by the court with prejudice.

- CAIR also sued Cass Ballenger for $2 million after the then-U.S. Congressman said in a 2003 interview with the *Charlotte Observer* that the group was a "fundraising arm for Hezbollah" that he had reported as such to the FBI and CIA. Fortunately, the judge ruled that Ballenger's statements were made in the scope of his public duties and were protected speech.

- A Muslim police officer is suing former CIA official and counterterrorism consultant Bruce Tefft and the New York Police Department for workplace harassment merely because Tefft sent emails with relevant news stories about Islamic terrorism to a voluntary list of recipients that included police officers.

These suits represent a direct and real threat to our constitutional rights and national security. Even if the lawsuits don't succeed, the continued use of lawfare tactics by Islamist organizations has the potential to create a detrimental chilling effect on public discourse and information concerning the war on terror.

Already, publishers have canceled books on the subject of counterterrorism and no doubt other journalists and authors have self-censored due to the looming threat of suit. For its part, CAIR announced an ambitious fundraising goal of $1 million, partly to "defend against defamatory attacks on Muslims and Islam." One of CAIR's staffers, Rabiah Ahmed, bragged[373] that lawsuits are increasingly an "instrument" for it to use.

U.S. courts have not yet grasped the importance of rebuffing international attempts to restrain the free speech rights of American citizens.

This is troubling. The United States was founded on the premise of freedom of worship, but also on the principle of the freedom to criticize religion. Islamists should not be allowed to stifle constitutionally protected speech, nor should they be allowed to subject innocent citizens who talk to other citizens about issues of national security to frivolous and costly lawsuits.

---

373 "Unmasking CAIR: Think Globally, Act Locally," by Andrew L. Jaffee, NetWMD.com, May 18, 2006. Available online at http://netwmd.com/blog/2006/05/18/550

APPENDIX B: MEMORANDA

On November 25, 2008, Brooke Goldstein addressed members of Parliament, by invitation of MP Patrick Mercer and hosted by the Henry Jackson Society. The following first two brief memoranda were circulated at that time to interested members of Parliament to assist them in deliberation, and were subsequently requested by members of the US Senate and House of Representatives. In turn, they formed the core of the third memorandum appearing herein, which was submitted to the British House of Commons Culture Media and Sports Committee in March of 2009, pursuant to its investigation into Press standards, privacy and libel.

BRIEF MEMORANDUM ADDRESSING PERTINENT DIFFERENCES BETWEEN US AND UK LIBEL LAW[374]

December 15, 2008

BURDEN OF PROVING TRUTH (OR FALSITY)

US: Plaintiff has burden of proving falsity of allegedly defamatory statement (truth of statement is presumed at law)

UK: Defendant has burden of proving truth of allegedly defamatory statement (falsity of statement is presumed at law)

FAULT STANDARD(S)

US: Distinction between public and private figures, with more protection for the latter. In cases of public figure, plaintiff must prove actual malice

UK: Uniform standard of fault; good reputation presumed for all plaintiffs, no need to prove actual malice

HEIGHTENED FAULT STANDARD FOR MATTERS OF PUBLIC CONCERN/PUBLIC INTEREST

US: On matters of public concern, plaintiffs must prove actual malice; "public concern" is construed broadly

UK: There is a qualified privilege ("responsible journalism"), but falsity and damage are presumed by law. If truth is not a possible defense, defendant must prove that it acted "responsibly" in attempting to discern truth of matter

---

374 Available online at http://www.legal-project.org/documents/221.doc

US: Presumptively invalid, under the 1st Amendment and jurisprudence

UK: Though there's a general rule against them, it is possible to submit a prepublication injunction request, to which defendant must assert that it will defend with a claim of truth, or other such substantive defense

RECOMMENDATIONS

* Switch legal presumption from falsity to presumption of truth, then shift the burden of proving the contrary on the plaintiff [This is the key element]

* Require showing of actual malice in cases involving public figures, and speech regarding matters of public concern

* Avoid potential misuse by sensationalist editors by incorporating American jurisprudential construction of "reckless disregard for the truth" into definition of "actual malice"

* Consider implementing anti-SLAPP laws to limit filing of malicious and chilling defamation suits aimed at silencing critics of oneself or organization. Include award of all costs to would-be SLAPP victim

* Introduce a bill designed to supersede previous Acts, including Defamation Act 1996 as far as they are affected by these changes

* Instruct British courts to decline jurisdiction in cases where their jurisdiction is clearly not the correct forum (i.e. a handful of copies of a book published elsewhere and suit brought by a non-resident)

A) Under applicable UK law, contempt is available in cases where a judgment was issued, and penalties for contempt may include committal. RSC Order 45, Rule 5(1)(b)(iii); CCR Order 29(1)

B) Failure to comply with a court order is enough to give rise to liability for contempt without a showing of specific intent to do the same. *Heatons Transport (St Helens) Ltd v. Transport and General Workers Union* [1973] AC 15, [1972] 3 All ER 101 at 117 (HL)

C) Under UK Law, service may be effected on foreign individuals visiting the UK for even the briefest of visits. *Colt Industries Inc v. Sarlic*[1966] 1 WLR 440 (CA); *Maharanee of Baroda v. Wildenstein* [1972] 2 QB 283 (CA)

D) Enforcement of a UK judgment may be requested in any EU nation, in the form of a European Enforcement Order. Commission Regulation (EC) No 1869/2005

When a person who has been ordered by a Court to either do[376] or abstain from doing[377] a particular act refuses or neglects to perform or refrains from performing said act, a judge can issue a writ of sequestration against the person's property[378] or an order of

---

375 Available online at http://www.legal-project.org/documents/222.doc
376 RSC Order 45 Rule 5(1)(a)
377 RSC Order 45 Rule 5(1)(b)
378 RSC Order 45 Rule 5(1)(b)(i)

committal.[379] [*See*, also, CCR Order 29 Rule 1(1)] While the Civil Procedure Rules indicate that committal should be an option of last resort, it remains a potential penalty for non-compliance.

British case law further supports the view that failure to comply with a court order can give rise to liability for contempt without a showing of specific intent.[380] The only requirement in this regard is that the non-complying person has been served with the judgment or order[381] or, in some circumstances, that the person has simply been notified of the judgment or order, by telephone, fax, email or otherwise.[382]

Setting aside for the moment the above provision that obviates the need for service of an order or judgment, British courts have consistently held that service may be made on foreign parties while visiting the United Kingdom, even on the briefest of visits.[383] Moreover, a foreign corporation, such as a publisher, that conducts business within the jurisdiction of British courts, by, for example, maintaining a fixed location within the UK or by employing a UK-based agent with authority to enter into contracts on behalf of the corporation, can be held to be a 'resident' under British law and, thus, subject to the authority of British courts.[384]

Accordingly, when a judgment or order has been issued against a publisher with sufficient business contacts in the United Kingdom, the publisher may also face penalties under the statutes

---

379 RSC Order 45 Rule 5(1)(b)(iii)

380 Heatons Transport (St Helens) Ltd v. Transport and General Workers Union [1973] AC 15, [1972] 3 All ER 101 at 117 (HL)

381 CCR Order 29 Rule 1(2)(a) & (b)

382 CCR Order 29 Rule 1(6)(b)

383 See, e.g. Colt Industries Inc v. Sarlic [1966] 1 WLR 440 (CA); Maharanee of Baroda v Wildenstein [1972] 2 QB 283 (CA)

384 Jabbour v Custodian of Absentee's Property for the State of Israel [1954] 1 All ER 145, [1954] 1 WLR 139

cited above, as well as an order of sequestration against any director or officer of the corporation.[385]

While this demonstrates how an American party, being either an individual author or a publishing corporation, who refuses to accept a British judgment may be penalized in the United Kingdom, based on minimal or even transitory contacts, the potential effects of a British judgment, default or otherwise, are more far-reaching still.

On November 16, 2005, the European Commission re-leased Commission Regulation (EC) No 1869/2005, which amended an earlier regulation[386]. This Regulation creates a mechanism throughout the European Union (EU) for the enforcement of uncontested claims brought in a member state. The aptly-named European Enforcement Orders effectively result in a wide-reaching web that allows for the enforcement of default judgments for pecuniary claims across the entire EU, excepting only Denmark.[387] Once a judgment has been certified as a European Enforcement Order, it "...shall be recognised and enforced in the other Member States without the need for a declaration of enforceability and without any possibility of opposing its recognition."[388]

As the preceding demonstrates, the mere non-enforcement by US courts of foreign defamation judgments is insufficient by itself to ensure that American authors and publishers benefit in practice from the First Amendment. Default judgments against US-based parties by UK courts, for example, can give rise to liability for contempt of court, with penalties that

---

385 RSC Order 45 Rule 5(1)(b)(ii)
386 Namely, European Regulation (EC) No 805/2004
387 European Regulation (EC) No 805/2004(5)
388 European Regulation (EC) No 805/2004 Chapter 2 Article 5

may, as has been shown, include committal. Travel by such parties, moreover, including individual authors and directors or officers of publishing houses, to the entire EU is adversely affected by virtue of the fact that a European Enforcement Order can be issued anywhere in the EU[389] demanding compliance with the financial aspect of the original court's ruling.

In summary, while Congressional measures to block the recognition and enforcement of foreign defamation judgments domestically are essential, the "chilling effect" of foreign lawsuits effectively precludes the individual from traveling anywhere in the EU, for fear of being held liable for the same foreign judgments that United States courts refuse to recognize for failure to comply with the protections of the First Amendment.

The essence of the American concept of free speech is that it is a fundamental natural right and that free and open discussion of important matters constitutes a powerful barrier against tyranny. When combined with potentially-adverse effects on US publishing corporations with considerable European business connections, the dangers of not responding to these predatory lawsuits by offensive legislation need scarcely be pointed out at length. To be blunt, a shield will stop an enemy from killing you, but it will not stop the enemy. Only a sword can accomplish that task.

---

389 With the sole exception of Denmark

MEMORANDUM SUBMITTED BY BROOKE M. GOLDSTEIN, DIRECTOR, THE LEGAL PROJECT AT THE MIDDLE EAST FORUM[390]

I. EXECUTIVE SUMMARY

1. Today, libel lawfare is being waged in the form of frivolous and malicious lawsuits designed to intimidate, silence and bankrupt anyone who speaks publicly about militant Islam, terrorism, or its sources of financing.

2. The United Kingdom's particular libel and jurisdictional statutes have made the UK the favored forum for these suits, which are creating a chilling effect on the exercise of free speech about matters of grave public concern not only within the UK, but throughout Europe and North America.

3. The continued use of British courts to silence American authors has prompted the New York State Senate to pass the Libel Terrorism Protection Act, and the Federal Government to consider for passage as law the Free Speech Protection Act, both which specifically nullifies foreign libel judgments against Americans sued in UK and other foreign courts. The effect of this law is to render impotent any British libel judgment against a US citizen should a US court render British law to provide inadequate protections for free speech as defined under the First Amendment of the United States' Constitution.

---

390 Submitted to the United Kingdom House of Commons Culture Media and Sports Committee, March 2009. Available online at
http://www.publications.parliament.uk/pa/cm200809/cmselect/cmcumeds/memo/press/ucps 4602.htm and http://www.legal-project.org/article/238

4. The continuing abuse of UK law seems to be reducing the nation's standing and otherwise impugning the UK's venerable reputation as a defender of freedom of speech and the due course of justice.

II. THE SUBMITTING PARTY: BROOKE GOLDSTEIN, DIRECTOR OF THE LEGAL PROJECT AT THE MIDDLE EAST FORUM

BROOKE GOLDSTEIN:

1. Brooke Goldstein is a licensed and practicing attorney based out of New York City and Philadelphia. Her expertise is in human rights law, specifically as it relates to the First Amendment of the US Constitution and the protection of free speech and free assembly. Goldstein also has a focus and is a recognized expert on the legalities surrounding children in armed conflict.

2. Goldstein has been invited to brief government officials at the U.S. State Department, the White House, and at U.S. Central Command, and has visited U.S. military bases and military schools to address US troops on issues of asymmetric warfare. In November of 2008 Goldstein was invited to brief members of the UK Parliament on the issue of libel lawfare and libel tourism.

3. Goldstein has published widely on the issue of libel tourism, UK libel law and libel lawfare, including, but not limited to the *American Spectator,* The *Middle East Quarterly, Counter Terrorist Magazine,* The *New York Daily News,* USINFO, FrontPage Magazine and other publications.

4. Goldstein is the 2007 recipient of the E. Nathaniel Gates Award for Outstanding Public Advocacy, the 2009 Inspire! Award bestowed by the Benjamin N Cardozo School of law, is an adjunct fellow at the Hudson Institute, a fellow at the Henry

Jackson Society, and serves as the Director of the Legal Project at the Middle East Forum.

5. Goldstein is also an award winning filmmaker, her most recent documentary film "The Making of a Martyr," about child suicide bombers, was honored in 2006 by the United Nations with the Audience Choice Award for Best Film and is currently broadcast on television stations throughout the globe, including in Canada, Sweden Korea and the Middle East.

6. Goldstein is a seasoned lecturer and has taught seminars at various graduate schools including the Benjamin N Cardozo School of Law, New York University, Berkeley University, and Stanford University.

7. Goldstein has made several media appearances including on FOX News, CNN, the John Batchelor Show, WABC News Talk Radio, TVE (of Spain), on RAI (of Italy), NYC TV (local ch.25), Time Warner's "Faith to Faith" television show (Brooke's episode won the Telly Award for Outstanding Programming).

8. As an effort to facilitate public awareness and fruitful discussion of human rights violations against children ignored by the mainstream media, Brooke co-founded A2B Film Productions Inc., a Canadian-based independent documentary film production company focused on creating films that expose and explore such issues.

9. Goldstein is also the founder and director of the Children's Rights Institute, a not for profit dedicated to raising awareness and legally combat the recruitment and incitement of children to become child soldiers, human shields and suicide bombers. [*See* www.childrensrightsinstitute.org]

10. The Legal Project at the Middle East Forum is a not-for-profit organization that operates similarly to a public interest law firm and which provides pro-bono and reduced rate legal representation to politicians, authors, activists and publishers targeted with strategic lawsuits designed to silence their exercise of free speech.

11. The mandate of the Legal Project has since expanded to encompass a response to attempts by Islamists targeting the human rights of North American and European civilians in order to constrain the free flow of public information about militant Islam, terrorism and its sources of financing.

12. The Legal Project is in the unique position of being completely dedicated to dealing with all facets of Lawfare, including the particular tactical manifestations thereof commonly referred to as "libel terrorism" or "libel tourism."

13. Due to its expertise, the Legal Project has been requested to submit memoranda and informational analysis to both the United States Congress and Parliament on the subjects of British contempt law and its effect on US citizens and comparative UK and US laws of defamation.

14. The Legal Project has also been involved in several high profile cases defending the rights of American and European citizens to speak freely on issues of public concern.

III. THE PHENOMENON OF LIBEL TOURISM IN THE UNITED KINGDOM, A MANIFESTATION OF 'LAWFARE' DESIGNED TO CURB PUBLIC DISCUSSION ABOUT ISSUES OF GRAVE PUBLIC CONCERN

15. Lawfare is defined as the use of the law as a weapon of war, or the pursuit of strategic aims through aggressive legal maneuvers.

16. Over the past ten years, we have seen a steady increase in lawfare tactics directly targeting the human rights of North American and European civilians in order to constrain the free flow of public information about militant Islam, terrorism and its sources of financing.

17. UK courts, due to the nature of British libel laws, principles of long arm jurisdiction, and "hate speech" legislation, have proved more friendly jurisdictions for parties who want to restrict the dissemination of material drawing attention to militant Islam and terror financing, and deemed 'blasphemous' of the Islamic religion due to their critical nature. Lawfare tactics have created a chilling effect on the exercise of free speech within the UK and the US.

IV. ISLAMIST LAWFARE: CASES AND CONTROVERSIES IN THE UNITED KINGDOM

18. A major player in the area of libel tourism is Khalid bin Mahfouz, a wealthy businessman who resides in Saudi Arabia and who has been accused by numerous parties of financially supporting Al Qaeda. Faced with the prospect of protracted and expensive litigation, a heavy burden of proof on the defendant, notoriously generous libel awards and the ability to recover costs, the majority of people who are merely threatened with lawsuit by Mahfouz and within the UK, regardless of the merit of their works, have issued apologies and retractions, while some have also paid fines and "contributions" to his charities.

19. In 2007, when Mahfouz threatened to sue Cambridge University Press for publishing the book *Alms for Jihad*, by Robert Collins and J Millard Burr, Cambridge Press immediately capitulated, offered a public apology to Mahfouz, took the book it once stood by out of print, pulped the unsold copies, and made

the outrageous demand that libraries all over the world remove the work from their shelves, a demand that was met with outright refusal and considerable derision.

20. Right after the US publication of Rachel Ehrenfeld's book entitled *Funding Evil*, Mahfouz sued Ehrenfeld for defamation because she too had written about financial ties between him and terrorist entities. The allegations against Ehrenfeld were heard by a UK court despite the fact that neither Mahfouz nor Ehrenfeld resides in England; the court asserted jurisdiction over her on the basis of approximately 23 copies of *Funding Evil* sold online to UK buyers via Amazon.com.

21. Unwilling to travel to England or to acknowledge the authority of English libel laws over herself and her work, Ehrenfeld lost on default and was ordered to pay heavy fines, apologize, and destroy her books, all of which she refused to do.

22. In response to Ehrenfeld's case, the New York State legislature and the United States House of Representatives unanimously passed the Libel Terrorism Protection Act and the Free Speech Protection Act respectively, which operate to expressly prohibit domestic judicial recognition of foreign libel judgments from jurisdictions with fewer protections for free speech then granted under the US Constitution.

23. Mohammad Sawalha, president of the British Muslim Initiative and a man who, according to a recent BBC documentary, coordinated funding for the EU designated terror group Hamas, launched a libel suit against the British blog Harry's Place, for accurately translating what may have been a mistranscription of an Al-Jazeera interview during which Sawalha allegedly referenced the "Jewish evil" in Britain. When Al-Jazeera amended the term to "Jewish lobby," Harry's Place responsibly reported the change in

an update. Sawalha, an activist for the anti-Semitic and hateful terrorist organization Hamas, was apparently objecting to the implication that he is "anti-Semitic and hateful".

24. Saudi billionaire and businessman Mohammed Jameel likewise took advantage of UK courts and sued the Wall Street Journal for libel over an article which reported about the Saudi Arabian authorities' monitoring of bank accounts, apparently including Jameel's, for evidence of supporting terrorism. Fortunately the British court, articulating the Reynolds doctrine, overturned Judge Eady, the same judge in Ehrenfeld's case, and held the article to be one of public importance and published responsibly.

25. When British television Channel 4 broadcast part one of an exposé of militant Islam in UK mosques, which showed extremist Imams engaging in anti-democratic rants and inciting the murder of British soldiers, the station was attacked by the West Midlands police force which accused the station, not the radical Imams, but the station of "damaging community relations" and reported Ch 4 to the Broadcasting Standards Commission, who attempted unsuccessfully, to prosecute them for 'racial hatred.'

26. When Christian Revelation Television hosted a guest speaker who expressed his opinion that Islam was not a religion of peace, OfCom judged the station to have violated Rule 4.1 of their Code, a particularly vague and ambiguous law requiring broadcasters of religious programs to steer away from material that "exploits the susceptibilities of religious audiences," which is equally nebulous and easily subject to manipulation. Revelation TV, instead of defending their right to free speech, groveled apologetically at the charge that they may have offended anyone.

27. This past June, a police community support officer ordered two Christian preachers to stop handing out gospel leaflets in a predominantly Muslim area of Birmingham. The evangelists were threatened with arrest for committing a "hate crime" by spreading their Christian message and telling Muslims youth to leave Islam, and were told they risked being beaten up if they returned."

28. The cumulative effect of the lawsuits, threatened actions, and seeming double standards above directly contributes to the silencing of free speech on a global scale, adversely affects the United Kingdom's reputation for upholding core democratic values, and provides a benefit only to those who callously manipulate the legal system in order to achieve their goals, which are fundamentally anti-democratic.

29. This manipulation of the legal system further adversely affects Anglo-American relations, including, but not limited to, traditional principles of comity between the two nations, and eats away at the Anglo-American legal tradition, a shared body of law and basic principles that is a cornerstone of modern civil law.

V. HATE SPEECH LAWS

30. Of course there is no such thing as the absolute freedom to speak, and there are indeed legitimate constraints on speech such as obscenity, defamation or incitement to immediate violence, yelling fire in a crowded theatre, and it is perfectly legitimate for anti-hate laws to be used to increase the punishment for crimes that are racially motivated.

31. However, when hate speech laws are selectively applied, when they are interpreted too liberally, or written too ambiguously, when they are used to criminalize satire or opinion or to punish merely what is offensive to some, or when hate speech

laws are used as a guise to enforce punishment of blasphemy, then they are being used to infringe the rights of the speaker who is neither afforded any type of due process or equal protection under the law. There is also the danger that hate speech laws provide a slippery slope downwards towards criminalizing legitimate actions and dialogue.

32. Moreover, the goals of those who seek to apply libel and hate speech laws to persons talking about terrorism or militant Islam are not to increase the peace, but to subvert discussion and knowledge about a very real danger and to undermine democratic values. Banning speech critical of religion is a step backwards, and banning speech about terrorism is a step towards legitimizing such violence. Secular laws must be designed to protect the free exercise of religion not blasphemy and a distinction must be drawn between for example, harassing someone on their way to pray and standing on a soap box and insulting Judaism, Christianity or Islam.

33. Legislators must work to draw a finer line between what is acceptable speech and what is not, what is protected opinion and satire and what is libel or incitement to violence against a religious group. By silencing dialogue about religion, terrorism and the role of religion in secular society, we are making it easier for radical elements to achieve their goals by robbing our societies of the ability to discuss real threats and by stifling our own intellectual powers to fight it.

34. Burden of proving truth (or falsity)

    a. <u>US</u>: Plaintiff has burden of proving falsity of allegedly defamatory statement (truth of statement is presumed at law)

    b. <u>UK</u>: Defendant has burden of proving truth of allegedly defamatory statement (falsity of statement is presumed at law)

35. Fault standard(s)

    c. <u>US</u>: Distinction between public and private figures, with more protection for the latter. In cases of public figure, plaintiff must prove actual malice

    d. <u>UK</u>: Uniform standard of fault; good reputation presumed for all plaintiffs, no need to prove actual malice

36. Heightened fault standard for matters of public concern/public interest

    e. <u>US</u>: On matters of public concern, plaintiffs must prove actual malice; "public concern" is construed broadly

    f. <u>UK</u>: There is a qualified privilege ("responsible journalism", Reynolds doctrine), but falsity and damage are presumed by law. If truth is not a possible defense, defendant must prove that it acted "responsibly" in attempting to discern truth of matter

37. Prior restraints

    g. <u>US</u>: Presumptively invalid, under the 1st Amendment and jurisprudence

    h. <u>UK</u>: Though there's a general rule against them, it is possible to submit a prepublication injunction request, to which defendant must assert that it will defend with a claim of truth, or other such substantive defense

VIII. RECOMMENDATIONS FOR ACTION BY THE GOVERNMENT

38. Convert the legal presumption in defamation cases from falsity to a presumption of truth, followed by shifting the burden of proving the contrary on the plaintiff.

39. Require a showing of actual malice in cases involving public figures, and speech regarding matters of public concern.

40. Avoid potential misuse by sensationalist editors by incorporating the American jurisprudential concept of "reckless disregard for the truth" into a definition of "actual malice," where, unlike the American definition, rather than a fault standard to apply to a class of people or issues, the actual malice requirement would prove a form of 'second tier' level of fault a plaintiff could plead, for which he or she could then recover additional damages against the unscrupulous and sensationalist 'journalist' who ignored facts in order to conduct a hatchet job.

41. Consider implementing anti-SLAPP [Strategic Lawsuit Against Public Participation] laws to limit the filing of malicious and chilling defamation suits aimed at silencing critics of oneself or organization. Include award of all costs to would-be SLAPP victim.

42. Introduce a bill designed to supersede previous Acts, including Defamation Act 1996 as far as they are affected by these changes

43. Instruct British courts to decline jurisdiction in cases where jurisdiction would clearly not represent the correct forum (i.e. a handful of copies of a book published elsewhere and suit brought by a non-resident).

44. Re-examine the application and prudency of "hate speech" laws and prevent their application as a guise for enforcing blasphemy laws.

45. Request the oral testimony of the following individuals:

a. **Brooke M. Goldstein**, director of the Legal Project at the Middle East Forum. In her capacity as Legal Project director, Ms. Goldstein has spent the past two years intensely involved with the study of Libel Lawfare, particularly as it pertains to freedom of speech in both a historical and current context.

b. **Andrew C. McCarthy**, director of the Center for Law and Counterterrorism at the Foundation for the Defense of Democracies. Mr. McCarthy is also a former Assistant United States Attorney for the Southern District of New York, during which time he was heavily involved in prosecuting terrorism.

c. **David B. Rivkin,** Jr., partner, the law firm of Baker Hostetler. Mr. Rivkin has considerable experience with, and expertise in, numerous United States constitutional issues, including those pertaining to the First Amendment, and is further experienced in the area of public international law.

APPENDIX C: STATES WITH ANTI-SLAPP STATUTES

A s detailed in Chapter 6, anti-SLAPP statutes afford additional protections for journalists writing on matters of public interest. The following is a list of states with anti-SLAPP statutes, including citation to applicable state codes.[391] Additionally, there are several organizations that are actively involved in anti-SLAPP legislation and/or protecting journalists, authors, bloggers, and others against legal reprisal. These include Harvard's Citizens Media Law Project (citmedialaw.org), California Anti-SLAPP Project (casp.net), and the Public Participation Project (anti-slapp.org). Neither the Center for Security Policy, nor the authors of this book, are affiliated with the above listed organizations which are mentioned purely for informational purposes.

---

391 This list was last updated on August 2011. For more up to date information on anti-SLAPP statutes, refer to the websites listed above.

Arizona: The Public Participation in Government Act. ARIZ. REV. STAT. ANN. §§ 12-751 - 12-752 (2009).

Arkansas: The Citizen Participation in Government Act. ARK. CODE ANN. §§ 16-63-501 - 16-63-508 (2009)

California: California's Claim Arising from Person's Exercise of Constitutional Right of Petition or Free Speech – Special Motion to Strike law, Cal. Civ. Proc. Code § 425.16 (2009-2010)

Delaware: Actions involving Public Petition and Participation, Standards for Motion to Dismiss and Summary Judgment in Certain Cases Involving Public Petition and Participation and Recovery of Damages in Actions Involving Public Petition and Participation. DEL. CODE. ANN. tit. 10 §§ 8136-8138 (2010).

Florida: Strategic Lawsuits Against Public Participation (SLAPP) suits by governmental entities prohibited, FLA. STAT. §768.295 (2010)

Right of owners to peaceably assemble; display of flag; SLAPP suits prohibited, FLA. STAT. § 720.304(4) (2010)

Georgia: Exercise of rights of freedom of speech and right to petition government for redress of grievances; legislative findings;

---

392 Prepared by Jacquelyn Kline (January 14, 2009, updated February 27, 2010.) A non-updated version of this list is available online at http://www.legal-project.org/article/149

verification of claims; definitions; procedure on motions; exception; attorney's fees and expenses, O.C.G.A. § 9-11-11.1. (2009)

Guam: Chapter 17: Citizen Participation in Government Act, 7 G.C.A. §§17101-17109 (2009)

Hawaii: Chapter 634F: Citizen Participation in Government Act, HAW. Rev. Stat Vol. 13 §§634F-1 – 634F-4 (2009)

Illinois: Chapter 735. Civil Procedure Citizen Participation Act, 735 ILL. COMP. STAT. 110/1, 110/5, 110/10, 110/15, 110/20, 110/25, 110/30, 110/35, 110/99 (2009)

Indiana: Chapter 7 Defense in Civil Actions Against Persons Who Act in Furtherance of the Person's Right of Petition or Free Speech Under the Constitution of the United States or the Constitution of the State of Indiana in Connection with a Public Issue, IND CODE §§ 34-7-7-1 – 34-7-7-10 (2009)

Louisiana: Special Motion To Strike, La. C.C.P. Art. 971 (2010)

Maine: Special Motion to Dismiss, 14 M.R.S. § 556 (2009)

Maryland: Strategic Lawsuits Against Public Participation, MD. CODE ANN. § 5-807 (2009)

Massachusetts: Special Motion to Dismiss Claim Based on Exercise of Constitutional Right of Petition, MASS. GEN. LAWS. ANN. ch. 231 § 59H (2009).

Minnesota: Declaratory, Corrective, Administrative Remedies. Free Speech; Participation in Government, Minn. Stat. § 554.01 (2009)

Missouri: Actions for damages for conduct or speech at public hearings and meetings to be considered on expedited basis -- procedural issues, MO. REV. STAT. § 537-528.1-7 (2009).

Nebraska: (bb) Public Petition And Participation, NEB. REV. STAT. §§ 25-21,241- 25-21,246 (2009)

Nevada: Liability of Persons Who Engage in Right to Petition, NEV. REV. STAT. §§ 41.635 – 41.670 (2009).

New Mexico: Special motion to dismiss unwarranted or specious lawsuits; procedures; sanctions; severability, N.M. STAT. ANN. § 38-2-9.1 (2009); Findings and purpose, N.M. STAT. ANN. §38-2-9.2 (2009).

New York: Actions involving public petition and participation, N.Y. CIV. RIGHTS 70-a (2009); Recovery of damages, N.Y. CIV. RIGHTS 76-a (2000); § 76-a; Motion to dismiss, N.Y. C.P.L.R 3211(g) (2009); R 3212. Motion for summary judgment, N.Y. C.P.L.R 3212(h) (2009)

Oklahoma: Privileged communication defined--Exemption from libel, OKLA. STAT. tit. 12, chap. 25 § 1443.1

Oregon: Special Motion To Strike, OR. REV. STAT. §§ 31.150 – 31.155 (2007)

Pennsylvania: Chapter 77. Costs And Fees, 27 PA. CONS. STAT §§ 7707 – 7708 (2009); Chapter 83. Participation In Environmental Law Or Regulation, 27 PA. CONS. STAT §§ 8301 – 8305 (2009)

Rhode Island: Chapter 33. Limits On Strategic Litigation Against Public Participation, R.I. GEN. LAWS §§ 9-33-1 – 9-33-4 (2009); Appeals -- Participation in zoning hearing, R.I. GEN. LAWS § 45-24-67 (2009)

Tennessee: Part 10 --Tennessee Anti-Slapp Act of 1997 -- Strategic Lawsuits Against Political Participation, TENN. CODE. ANN. §§ 4-21-1001 – 4-21-1004 (2009)

Utah: PART 14. Citizen Participation In Government Act, UTAH CODE ANN. §§ 78B-6-1401 – 78B-6-1405 (2009)

Vermont: Exercise of rights to free speech and to petition government for redress of grievances; special motion to strike, 12 V.S.A. §1041 (2009).

Washington: Good faith communication to government agency -- When agency or attorney general may defend against lawsuit -- Costs and fees, WASH. REV. CODE § 4.24.520 (2009)

STATES WITH JUDICIAL DOCTRINE ON SLAPPS (NO STATUTE)

West Virginia: There was no evidence of anti-SLAPP bills, but there have been several cases. *Webb v. Fury* (282 S.E.2d 28); *Harris v. Adkins* (432 S.E.2d 549)

STATES WITH ANTI-SLAPP BILLS (CURRENT OR PREVIOUS)

Colorado: Colorado's Sixty-third General Assembly's House Bill 02-1192 was introduced in 2002. The bill was read three times, with the third reading effectively stalling the bill.

Connecticut: Connecticut's 1991 Raised Bill 7374 and 1993 House Bill 1026, Senate Bill 182, and Senate Bill 248 all failed.

Kansas: Kansas' 1997 Senate Bill No. 287 was pulled by Senator Clark in March of 1998 because the proposed amendments by the state bar association would have made the bill essentially non-effective.

Michigan: Senate Bill 1195 was introduced in May of 2004. House Bill 4709 was introduced in April 29, 1997 and referred to the Consumer Protection Committee, where a substitute bill was referred to the Judiciary Committee. However, the bill was never taken up by the Judiciary Committee.

New Hampshire: Senate Bill 661 was introduced in 1994. The state senate then requested the state supreme court's opinion whether the bill was consistent with the state constitution. The court responded that it was not. Opinion of the Justices (SLAPP Suit Procedure)(641 A.2d 1012)

New Jersey: New Jersey does not have an anti-SLAPP statute, although there were bills introduced in 1998 (Senate Bill No. 745) and in 1996 (Assembly Bill 1545). However, the New Jersey Courts have been sympathetic to those impacted by SLAPPs. As a result, the courts have allowed a defendant who successfully defeats a SLAPP-type suit to seek damages from the SLAPP filer on a claim of malicious use of process.

South Carolina: South Carolina's General Assembly, 118th Session, 2009-2010, Introduced the Citizens Participation in Government Act, H.3587 in the House on February 19, 2009. The Act is currently residing in the House Committee on Judiciary.

Texas: Civil Actions Against Persons Filing Complaints With Governmental Agencies Or Quasi-Governmental Entities, H.B. No. 1338. The bill was considered in a formal meeting in May of 2009 and reported favorably without amendments. The current status is unknown.

Virginia: Virginia's Senate Bill 424 from 1992 and 1993 failed.

Wisconsin: The Wisconsin House bill 946, the "Whistleblower Protection Act", was passed on September 23, 2009. However, the act failed to pass pursuant to Senate Joint Resolution 1.

Wyoming: Strategic Litigation Against Public Participation, HB0033, 07LSO-0190 (2007). The House Committee returned Bill pursuant to HR4.

NOTE: NO INFORMATION ON NORTH CAROLINA WAS LOCATED.

APPENDIX D: RELEVANT
LEGAL DOCUMENTS

This book refers to a number of primary legal materials, and includes links to these materials online wherever possible. There are, however, three legal documents that are so integral to the subject of this book that they are included here as an appendix. These documents are: (1) The Constitution of the United States of America; (2) The Universal Declaration of Human Rights; and (3) The Cairo Declaration on Human Rights in Islam.

THE CONSTITUTION OF THE UNITED STATES OF AMERICA

PREAMBLE

We the People of the United States, in Order to form a more perfect Union, establish Justice, insure domestic Tranquility, provide for the common defence, promote the general Welfare, and secure the Blessings of Liberty to ourselves and our Posterity, do ordain and establish this Constitution for the United States of America.

Article. I.

SECTION. 1. All legislative Powers herein granted shall be vested in a Congress of the United States, which shall consist of a Senate and House of Representatives.

SECTION. 2. The House of Representatives shall be composed of Members chosen every second Year by the People of the several States, and the Electors in each State shall have the Qualifications requisite for Electors of the most numerous Branch of the State Legislature.

No Person shall be a Representative who shall not have attained to the Age of twenty five Years, and been seven Years a Citizen of the United States, and who shall not, when elected, be an Inhabitant of that State in which he shall be chosen.

Representatives and direct Taxes shall be apportioned among the several States which may be included within this Union, according to their respective Numbers, which shall be determined by adding to the whole Number of free Persons, including those bound to Service for a Term of Years, and excluding Indians not taxed, three fifths of all other Persons. The actual Enumeration shall be made within three Years after the first Meeting of the Congress of the United States, and within every subsequent Term of ten Years, in such Manner as they shall by Law direct. The Number of Representatives shall not exceed one for every thirty Thousand, but each State shall have at Least one Representative; and until such enumeration shall be made, the State of New Hampshire shall be entitled to chuse three, Massachusetts eight, Rhode-Island and Providence Plantations one, Connecticut five, New-York six, New Jersey four, Pennsylvania eight, Delaware one, Maryland six, Virginia ten, North Carolina five, South Carolina five, and Georgia three.

When vacancies happen in the Representation from any State, the Executive Authority thereof shall issue Writs of Election to fill such Vacancies.

The House of Representatives shall chuse their Speaker and other Officers; and shall have the sole Power of Impeachment.

SECTION. 3. The Senate of the United States shall be composed of two Senators from each State, chosen by the Legislature thereof, for six Years; and each Senator shall have one Vote.

Immediately after they shall be assembled in Consequence of the first Election, they shall be divided as equally as may be into three Classes. The Seats of the Senators of the first Class shall be vacated at the Expiration of the second Year, of the second Class at the Expiration of the fourth Year, and of the third Class at the Expiration of the sixth Year, so that one third may be chosen every second Year; and if Vacancies happen by Resignation, or otherwise, during the Recess of the Legislature of any State, the Executive thereof may make temporary Appointments until the next Meeting of the Legislature, which shall then fill such Vacancies.

No Person shall be a Senator who shall not have attained to the Age of thirty Years, and been nine Years a Citizen of the United States, and who shall not, when elected, be an Inhabitant of that State for which he shall be chosen.

The Vice President of the United States shall be President of the Senate, but shall have no Vote, unless they be equally divided.

The Senate shall chuse their other Officers, and also a President pro tempore, in the Absence of the Vice President, or when he shall exercise the Office of President of the United States.

The Senate shall have the sole Power to try all Impeachments. When sitting for that Purpose, they shall be on Oath or Affirmation. When the President of the United States is tried, the Chief Justice shall preside: And no Person shall be convicted without the Concurrence of two thirds of the Members present.

Judgment in Cases of Impeachment shall not extend further than to removal from Office, and disqualification to hold and enjoy any Office of honor, Trust or Profit under the United States: but the Party convicted shall nevertheless be liable and subject to Indictment, Trial, Judgment and Punishment, according to Law.

SECTION. 4. The Times, Places and Manner of holding Elections for Senators and Representatives, shall be prescribed in each State by the Legislature thereof; but the Congress may at any time by Law make or alter such Regulations, except as to the Places of chusing Senators.

The Congress shall assemble at least once in every Year, and such Meeting shall be on the first Monday in December [Modified by Amendment XX], unless they shall by Law appoint a different Day.

SECTION. 5. Each House shall be the Judge of the Elections, Returns and Qualifications of its own Members, and a Majority of each shall constitute a Quorum to do Business; but a smaller Number may adjourn from day to day, and may be authorized to compel the Attendance of absent Members, in such Manner, and under such Penalties as each House may provide.

Each House may determine the Rules of its Proceedings, punish its Members for disorderly Behaviour, and, with the Concurrence of two thirds, expel a Member.

Each House shall keep a Journal of its Proceedings, and from time to time publish the same, excepting such Parts as may in their Judgment require Secrecy; and the Yeas and Nays of the Members of either House on any question shall, at the Desire of one fifth of those Present, be entered on the Journal.

Neither House, during the Session of Congress, shall, without the Consent of the other, adjourn for more than three days, nor to any other Place than that in which the two Houses shall be sitting.

SECTION. 6. The Senators and Representatives shall receive a Compensation for their Services, to be ascertained by Law, and paid out of the Treasury of the United States. They shall in all Cases, except Treason, Felony and Breach of the Peace, be privileged from Arrest during their Attendance at the Session of their respective Houses, and in going to and returning from the same; and for any Speech or Debate in either House, they shall not be questioned in any other Place.

No Senator or Representative shall, during the Time for which he was elected, be appointed to any civil Office under the Authority of the United States, which shall have been created, or the Emoluments whereof shall have been encreased during such time; and no Person holding any Office under the United States, shall be a Member of either House during his Continuance in Office.

SECTION. 7. All Bills for raising Revenue shall originate in the House of Representatives; but the Senate may propose or concur with Amendments as on other Bills.

Every Bill which shall have passed the House of Representatives and the Senate, shall, before it become a Law, be presented to the President of the United States; If he approve he shall sign it, but if not he shall return it, with his Objections to that House in which it shall have originated, who shall enter the Objections at large on their Journal, and proceed to reconsider it. If after such Reconsideration two thirds of that House shall agree to pass the Bill, it shall be sent, together with the Objections, to the other House, by which it shall likewise be reconsidered, and if approved by two thirds of that House, it shall become a Law. But in all such Cases the Votes of both Houses shall be determined by yeas and Nays, and the Names of the Persons voting for and against the Bill shall be entered on the Journal of each House respectively. If any Bill shall not be returned by the President within ten Days (Sundays excepted) after it shall have been presented to him, the Same shall be a Law, in like Manner as if he had signed it, unless the Congress by their Adjournment prevent its Return, in which Case it shall not be a Law.

Every Order, Resolution, or Vote to which the Concurrence of the Senate and House of Representatives may be necessary (except on a question of Adjournment) shall be presented to the President of the United States; and before the Same shall take Effect, shall be approved by him, or being disapproved by him, shall be repassed by two thirds of the Senate and House of Representatives, according to the Rules and Limitations prescribed in the Case of a Bill.

SECTION. 8. The Congress shall have Power To lay and collect Taxes, Duties, Imposts and Excises, to pay the Debts and provide for the common Defence and general Welfare of the United States; but all Duties, Imposts and Excises shall be uniform throughout the United States;

To borrow Money on the credit of the United States;

To regulate Commerce with foreign Nations, and among the several States, and with the Indian Tribes;

To establish an uniform Rule of Naturalization, and uniform Laws on the subject of Bankruptcies throughout the United States;

To coin Money, regulate the Value thereof, and of foreign Coin, and fix the Standard of Weights and Measures;

To provide for the Punishment of counterfeiting the Securities and current Coin of the United States;

To establish Post Offices and post Roads;

To promote the Progress of Science and useful Arts, by securing for limited Times to Authors and Inventors the exclusive Right to their respective Writings and Discoveries;

To constitute Tribunals inferior to the supreme Court;

To define and punish Piracies and Felonies committed on the high Seas, and Offences against the Law of Nations;

To declare War, grant Letters of Marque and Reprisal, and make Rules concerning Captures on Land and Water;

To raise and support Armies, but no Appropriation of Money to that Use shall be for a longer Term than two Years;

To provide and maintain a Navy;

To make Rules for the Government and Regulation of the land and naval Forces;

To provide for calling forth the Militia to execute the Laws of the Union, suppress Insurrections and repel Invasions;

To provide for organizing, arming, and disciplining, the Militia, and for governing such Part of them as may be employed in the Service of the United States, reserving to the States respectively, the Appointment of the Officers, and the Authority of training the Militia according to the discipline prescribed by Congress;

To exercise exclusive Legislation in all Cases whatsoever, over such District (not exceeding ten Miles square) as may, by

Cession of particular States, and the Acceptance of Congress, become the Seat of the Government of the United States, and to exercise like Authority over all Places purchased by the Consent of the Legislature of the State in which the Same shall be, for the Erection of Forts, Magazines, Arsenals, dock-Yards, and other needful Buildings; —And

To make all Laws which shall be necessary and proper for carrying into Execution the foregoing Powers, and all other Powers vested by this Constitution in the Government of the United States, or in any Department or Officer thereof.

SECTION. 9. The Migration or Importation of such Persons as any of the States now existing shall think proper to admit, shall not be prohibited by the Congress prior to the Year one thousand eight hundred and eight, but a Tax or duty may be imposed on such Importation, not exceeding ten dollars for each Person.

The Privilege of the Writ of Habeas Corpus shall not be suspended, unless when in Cases of Rebellion or Invasion the public Safety may require it.

No Bill of Attainder or ex post facto Law shall be passed.

No Capitation, or other direct, Tax shall be laid, unless in Proportion to the Census or Enumeration herein before directed to be taken.

No Tax or Duty shall be laid on Articles exported from any State.

No Preference shall be given by any Regulation of Commerce or Revenue to the Ports of one State over those of another; nor shall Vessels bound to, or from, one State, be obliged to enter, clear, or pay Duties in another.

No Money shall be drawn from the Treasury, but in Consequence of Appropriations made by Law; and a regular Statement and Account of the Receipts and Expenditures of all public Money shall be published from time to time.

No Title of Nobility shall be granted by the United States: And no Person holding any Office of Profit or Trust under them, shall, without the Consent of the Congress, accept of any present, Emolument, Office, or Title, of any kind whatever, from any King, Prince, or foreign State.

SECTION. 10. No State shall enter into any Treaty, Alliance, or Confederation; grant Letters of Marque and Reprisal; coin Money; emit Bills of Credit; make any Thing but gold and silver Coin a Tender in Payment of Debts; pass any Bill of Attainder, ex post facto Law, or Law impairing the Obligation of Contracts, or grant any Title of Nobility.

No State shall, without the Consent of the Congress, lay any Imposts or Duties on Imports or Exports, except what may be absolutely necessary for executing it's inspection Laws; and the net Produce of all Duties and Imposts, laid by any State on Imports or Exports, shall be for the Use of the Treasury of the United States; and all such Laws shall be subject to the Revision and Controul of the Congress.

No State shall, without the Consent of Congress, lay any Duty of Tonnage, keep Troops, or Ships of War in time of Peace, enter into any Agreement or Compact with another State, or with a foreign Power, or engage in War, unless actually invaded, or in such imminent Danger as will not admit of delay.

Article. II.

SECTION. 1. The executive Power shall be vested in a President of the United States of America. He shall hold his Office during the Term of four Years, and, together with the Vice President, chosen for the same Term, be elected, as follows:

Each State shall appoint, in such Manner as the Legislature thereof may direct, a Number of Electors, equal to the whole Number of Senators and Representatives to which the State may be entitled in the Congress: but no Senator or Representative, or

Person holding an Office of Trust or Profit under the United States, shall be appointed an Elector.

The Electors shall meet in their respective States, and vote by Ballot for two Persons, of whom one at least shall not be an Inhabitant of the same State with themselves. And they shall make a List of all the Persons voted for, and of the Number of Votes for each; which List they shall sign and certify, and transmit sealed to the Seat of the Government of the United States, directed to the President of the Senate. The President of the Senate shall, in the Presence of the Senate and House of Representatives, open all the Certificates, and the Votes shall then be counted. The Person having the greatest Number of Votes shall be the President, if such Number be a Majority of the whole Number of Electors appointed; and if there be more than one who have such Majority, and have an equal Number of Votes, then the House of Representatives shall immediately chuse by Ballot one of them for President; and if no Person have a Majority, then from the five highest on the List the said House shall in like Manner chuse the President. But in chusing the President, the Votes shall be taken by States, the Representation from each State having one Vote; a quorum for this Purpose shall consist of a Member or Members from two thirds of the States, and a Majority of all the States shall be necessary to a Choice. In every Case, after the Choice of the President, the Person having the greatest Number of Votes of the Electors shall be the Vice President. But if there should remain two or more who have equal Votes, the Senate shall chuse from them by Ballot the Vice President.

The Congress may determine the Time of chusing the Electors, and the Day on which they shall give their Votes; which Day shall be the same throughout the United States.

No Person except a natural born Citizen, or a Citizen of the United States, at the time of the Adoption of this Constitution, shall be eligible to the Office of President; neither shall any Person be eligible to that Office who shall not have attained to the Age of thirty five Years, and been fourteen Years a Resident within the United States.

In Case of the Removal of the President from Office, or of his Death, Resignation, or Inability to discharge the Powers and Duties of the said Office, the Same shall devolve on the Vice President, and the Congress may by Law provide for the Case of Removal, Death, Resignation or Inability, both of the President and Vice President, declaring what Officer shall then act as President, and such Officer shall act accordingly, until the Disability be removed, or a President shall be elected.

The President shall, at stated Times, receive for his Services, a Compensation, which shall neither be increased nor diminished during the Period for which he shall have been elected, and he shall not receive within that Period any other Emolument from the United States, or any of them.

Before he enter on the Execution of his Office, he shall take the following Oath or Affirmation: — "I do solemnly swear (or affirm) that I will faithfully execute the Office of President of the United States, and will to the best of my Ability, preserve, protect and defend the Constitution of the United States."

SECTION. 2. The President shall be Commander in Chief of the Army and Navy of the United States, and of the Militia of the several States, when called into the actual Service of the United States; he may require the Opinion, in writing, of the principal Officer in each of the executive Departments, upon any Subject relating to the Duties of their respective Offices, and he shall have Power to grant Reprieves and Pardons for Offences against the United States, except in Cases of Impeachment.

He shall have Power, by and with the Advice and Consent of the Senate, to make Treaties, provided two thirds of the Senators present concur; and he shall nominate, and by and with the Advice and Consent of the Senate, shall appoint Ambassadors, other public Ministers and Consuls, Judges of the supreme Court, and all other Officers of the United States, whose Appointments are not herein otherwise provided for, and which shall be established by Law: but the Congress may by Law vest the Appointment of such inferior Officers, as they think proper, in the President alone, in the Courts of Law, or in the Heads of Departments.

The President shall have Power to fill up all Vacancies that may happen during the Recess of the Senate, by granting Commissions which shall expire at the End of their next Session.

SECTION. 3. He shall from time to time give to the Congress Information of the State of the Union, and recommend to their Consideration such Measures as he shall judge necessary and expedient; he may, on extraordinary Occasions, convene both Houses, or either of them, and in Case of Disagreement between them, with Respect to the Time of Adjournment, he may adjourn them to such Time as he shall think proper; he shall receive Ambassadors and other public Ministers; he shall take Care that the Laws be faithfully executed, and shall Commission all the Officers of the United States.

SECTION. 4. The President, Vice President and all civil Officers of the United States, shall be removed from Office on Impeachment for, and Conviction of, Treason, Bribery, or other high Crimes and Misdemeanors.

Article. III.

SECTION. 1. The judicial Power of the United States shall be vested in one supreme Court, and in such inferior Courts as the Congress may from time to time ordain and establish. The Judges, both of the supreme and inferior Courts, shall hold their Offices during good Behaviour, and shall, at stated Times, receive for their Services a Compensation, which shall not be diminished during their Continuance in Office.

SECTION. 2. The judicial Power shall extend to all Cases, in Law and Equity, arising under this Constitution, the Laws of the United States, and Treaties made, or which shall be made, under their Authority; — to all Cases affecting Ambassadors, other public Ministers and Consuls; — to all Cases of admiralty and maritime Jurisdiction; — to Controversies to which the United States shall be a Party; — to Controversies between two or more States; — between a State and Citizens of another State; — between Citizens of different States; — between Citizens of the same State claiming Lands under Grants of different States, and between a State, or the Citizens thereof, and foreign States, Citizens or Subjects.

In all Cases affecting Ambassadors, other public Ministers and Consuls, and those in which a State shall be Party, the supreme Court shall have original Jurisdiction. In all the other Cases before mentioned, the supreme Court shall have appellate Jurisdiction, both as to Law and Fact, with such Exceptions, and under such Regulations as the Congress shall make.

The Trial of all Crimes, except in Cases of Impeachment, shall be by Jury; and such Trial shall be held in the State where the said Crimes shall have been committed; but when not committed within any State, the Trial shall be at such Place or Places as the Congress may by Law have directed.

SECTION. 3. Treason against the United States shall consist only in levying War against them, or in adhering to their Enemies, giving them Aid and Comfort. No Person shall be convicted of Treason unless on the Testimony of two Witnesses to the same overt Act, or on Confession in open Court.

The Congress shall have Power to declare the Punishment of Treason, but no Attainder of Treason shall work Corruption of Blood, or Forfeiture except during the Life of the Person attainted.

Article. IV.

SECTION. 1. Full Faith and Credit shall be given in each State to the public Acts, Records, and judicial Proceedings of every other State. And the Congress may by general Laws prescribe the Manner in which such Acts, Records and Proceedings shall be proved, and the Effect thereof.

SECTION. 2. The Citizens of each State shall be entitled to all Privileges and Immunities of Citizens in the several States.

A Person charged in any State with Treason, Felony, or other Crime, who shall flee from Justice, and be found in another State, shall on Demand of the executive Authority of the State from which he fled, be delivered up, to be removed to the State having Jurisdiction of the Crime.

No Person held to Service or Labour in one State, under the Laws thereof, escaping into another, shall, in Consequence of any Law or Regulation therein, be discharged from such Service or Labour, but shall be delivered up on Claim of the Party to whom such Service or Labour may be due.

SECTION. 3. New States may be admitted by the Congress into this Union; but no new State shall be formed or erected within the Jurisdiction of any other State; nor any State be formed by the Junction of two or more States, or Parts of States, without the Consent of the Legislatures of the States concerned as well as of the Congress.

The Congress shall have Power to dispose of and make all needful Rules and Regulations respecting the Territory or other Property belonging to the United States; and nothing in this Constitution shall be so construed as to Prejudice any Claims of the United States, or of any particular State.

SECTION. 4. The United States shall guarantee to every State in this Union a Republican Form of Government, and shall protect each of them against Invasion; and on Application of the Legislature, or of the Executive (when the Legislature cannot be convened), against domestic Violence.

Article. V.

The Congress, whenever two thirds of both Houses shall deem it necessary, shall propose Amendments to this Constitution, or, on the Application of the Legislatures of two thirds of the several States, shall call a Convention for proposing Amendments, which, in either Case, shall be valid to all Intents and Purposes, as Part of this Constitution, when ratified by the Legislatures of three fourths of the several States, or by Conventions in three fourths thereof, as the one or the other Mode of Ratification may be proposed by the Congress; Provided that no Amendment which may be made prior to the Year One thousand eight hundred and eight shall in any Manner affect the first and fourth Clauses in the Ninth Section of the first Article; and that no State, without its Consent, shall be deprived of its equal Suffrage in the Senate.

Article. VI.

All Debts contracted and Engagements entered into, before the Adoption of this Constitution, shall be as valid against the United States under this Constitution, as under the Confederation.

This Constitution, and the Laws of the United States which shall be made in Pursuance thereof; and all Treaties made, or which shall be made, under the Authority of the United States, shall be the supreme Law of the Land; and the Judges in every State shall be bound thereby, any Thing in the Constitution or Laws of any State to the Contrary notwithstanding.

The Senators and Representatives before mentioned, and the Members of the several State Legislatures, and all executive and judicial Officers, both of the United States and of the several States, shall be bound by Oath or Affirmation, to support this

Constitution; but no religious Test shall ever be required as a Qualification to any Office or public Trust under the United States.

Article. VII.

The Ratification of the Conventions of nine States, shall be sufficient for the Establishment of this Constitution between the States so ratifying the Same.

AMENDMENTS TO THE CONSTITUTION OF THE UNITED STATES

Amendment I

Congress shall make no law respecting an establishment of religion, or prohibiting the free exercise thereof; or abridging the freedom of speech, or of the press; or the right of the people peaceably to assemble, and to petition the Government for a redress of grievances.

Amendment II

A well regulated militia, being necessary to the security of a free State, the right of the people to keep and bear arms, shall not be infringed.

Amendment III

No soldier shall, in time of peace be quartered in any house, without the consent of the owner, nor in time of war, but in a manner to be prescribed by law.

Amendment IV

The right of the people to be secure in their persons, houses, papers, and effects, against unreasonable searches and seizures, shall not be violated, and no warrants shall issue, but upon probable cause, supported by oath or affirmation, and particularly describing the place to be searched, and the persons or things to be seized.

Amendment V

No person shall be held to answer for a capital, or otherwise infamous crime, unless on a presentment or indictment of a Grand Jury, except in cases arising in the land or naval forces, or in the militia, when in actual service in time of war or public danger; nor shall any person be subject for the same offence to be twice put in jeopardy of life or limb; nor shall be compelled in any criminal case to be a witness, against himself, nor be deprived of life, liberty, or property, without due process of law; nor shall private property be taken for public use, without just compensation.

Amendment VI

In all criminal prosecutions, the accused shall enjoy the right to a speedy and public trial, by an impartial jury of the State and district wherein the crime shall have been committed, which district shall have been previously ascertained by law, and to be informed of the nature and cause of the accusation; to be confronted with the witnesses against him; to have compulsory process for obtaining witnesses in his favor, and to have the assistance of counsel for his defense.

Amendment VII

In suits at common law, where the value in controversy shall exceed twenty dollars, the right of trial by jury shall be preserved, and no fact tried by a jury, shall be otherwise re-examined in any court of the United States, than according to the rules of the common law.

Amendment VIII

Excessive bail shall not be required, nor excessive fines imposed, nor cruel and unusual punishments inflicted.

Amendment IX

The enumeration in the Constitution, of certain rights, shall not be construed to deny or disparage others retained by the people.

Amendment X

The powers not delegated to the United States by the Constitution, nor prohibited by it to the States, are reserved to the States, respectively, or to the people.

Amendment XI

The judicial power of the United States shall not be construed to extend to any suit in law or equity, commenced or prosecuted against one of the United States by citizens of another State, or by citizens or subjects of any foreign state.

Amendment XII

The electors shall meet in their respective states, and vote by ballot for President and Vice President, one of whom, at least, shall not be an inhabitant of the same state with themselves; they shall name in their ballots the person voted for as President, and in distinct ballots the person voted for as Vice President, and they shall make distinct lists of all persons voted for as President, and of all persons voted for as Vice President, and of the number of votes for each, which lists they shall sign and certify, and transmit sealed to the seat of the government of the United States, directed to the President of the Senate; the President of the Senate shall, in the presence of the Senate and House of Representatives, open all the certificates and the votes shall then be counted; the person having the greatest number of votes for President, shall be the President, if such number be a majority of the whole number of electors appointed; and if no person have such majority, then from the persons having the highest numbers not exceeding three on the list of those voted for as President, the House of Representatives shall choose immediately, by ballot, the President. But in choosing the President, the votes shall be taken by states, the representation from each State having one vote; a quorum for this purpose shall consist of a member or members from two thirds of the states, and a majority of all the states shall be necessary to a choice. And if the House of Representatives shall not choose a President whenever the right of choice shall devolve upon them, before the fourth day of March next following, then the Vice President shall act as President, as in the case of the death or other constitutional disability of the President. The person having the greatest number of votes as Vice President, shall be the Vice President, if such number be a majority of the whole number of electors appointed, and if no person have a majority, then from the two highest numbers on the list, the Senate shall choose the Vice President; a quorum for the purpose shall consist of two thirds of the whole number of Senators, and a majority of the whole number shall be necessary to a choice. But no person constitutionally ineligible to the office of President shall be eligible to that of Vice President of the United States.

Amendment XIII

SECTION. 1. Neither slavery nor involuntary servitude, except as a punishment for crime whereof the party shall have been duly convicted, shall exist within the United States, or any place subject to their jurisdiction.

SECTION. 2. Congress shall have power to enforce this article by appropriate legislation.

Amendment XIV

SECTION. 1. All persons born or naturalized in the United States, and subject to the jurisdiction thereof, are citizens of the United States and of the State wherein they reside. No State shall make or enforce any law which shall abridge the privileges or immunities of citizens of the United States; nor shall any State deprive any person of life, liberty, or property, without due process of law; nor deny to any person within its jurisdiction the equal protection of the laws.

SECTION. 2. Representatives shall be apportioned among the several States according to their respective numbers, counting the whole number of persons in each State, excluding Indians not taxed. But when the right to vote at any election for the choice of electors for President and Vice President of the United States, Representatives in Congress, the executive and judicial officers of a State, or the members of the Legislature thereof, is denied to any of the male inhabitants of such State, being twenty-one years of age, and citizens of the United States, or in any way abridged, except for participation in rebellion, or other crime, the basis of representation therein shall be reduced in the proportion which the number of such male citizens shall bear to the whole number of male citizens twenty-one years of age in such State.

SECTION. 3. No person shall be a Senator or Representative in Congress, or elector of President and Vice President, or hold any office, civil or military, under the United States, or under any State, who, having previously taken an oath, as a member of Congress, or as an officer of the United States, or as a member of any State Legislature, or as an executive or judicial officer of any State, to support the Constitution of the United States, shall have engaged in insurrection or rebellion against the same, or given aid or comfort to the enemies thereof. But Congress may, by a vote of two thirds of each House, remove such disability.

SECTION. 4. The validity of the public debt of the United States, authorized by law, including debts incurred for payment of pensions and bounties for services in suppressing insurrection or rebellion, shall not be questioned. But neither the United States nor any State shall assume or pay any debt or obligation incurred in aid of insurrection or rebellion against the United States, or any claim for the loss or emancipation of any slave; but all such debts, obligations, and claims shall be held illegal and void.

SECTION. 5. The Congress shall have power to enforce, by appropriate legislation, the provisions of this article.

Amendment XV

SECTION. 1. The right of citizens of the United States to vote shall not be denied or abridged by the United States or by any State on account of race, color, or previous condition of servitude.

SECTION. 2. The Congress shall have power to enforce this article by appropriate legislation.

Amendment XVI

The Congress shall have power to lay and collect taxes on incomes, from whatever source derived, without apportionment among the several States, and without regard to any census or enumeration.

Amendment XVII

The Senate of the United States shall be composed of two Senators from each State, elected by the people thereof, for six years; and each Senator shall have one vote. The electors in each State shall have the qualifications requisite for electors of the most numerous branch of the State Legislatures.

When vacancies happen in the representation of any State in the Senate, the executive authority of such State shall issue writs of election to fill such vacancies: Provided, that the legislature of any State may empower the executive thereof to make temporary appointment until the people fill the vacancies by election as the legislature may direct.

This amendment shall not be so construed as to affect the election or term of any Senator chosen before it becomes valid as part of the Constitution.

Amendment XVIII

SECTION. 1. After one year from the ratification of this article the manufacture, sale, or transportation of intoxicating liquors within, the importation thereof into, or the exportation thereof from the United States and all territory subject to the jurisdiction thereof for beverage purposes is hereby prohibited.

SECTION. 2. The Congress and the several States shall have concurrent power to enforce this article by appropriate legislation.

SECTION. 3. This article shall be inoperative unless it shall have been ratified as an amendment to the Constitution by the legislatures of the several States, as provided in the Constitution, within seven years from the date of the submission hereof to the States by Congress.

Amendment XIX

The right of citizens of the United States to vote shall not be denied or abridged by the United States or by any State on account of sex.

Congress shall have power to enforce this article by appropriate legislation.

Amendment XX

SECTION. 1. The terms of the President and Vice President shall end at noon on the twentieth day of January, and the terms of Senators and Representatives at noon on the third day of January, of the years in which such terms would have ended if this article had not been ratified; and the terms of their successors shall then begin.

SECTION. 2. The Congress shall assemble at least once in every year, and such meeting shall begin at noon on the third day of January, unless they shall by law appoint a different day.

SECTION. 3. If, at the time fixed for the beginning of the term of the President, the President-elect shall have died, the Vice President-elect shall become President. If a President shall not have been chosen before the time fixed for the beginning of his term, or if the President-elect shall have failed to qualify, then the Vice President shall have qualified; and the Congress may by law provide for the case wherein neither a President-elect nor a Vice President-elect shall have qualified, declaring who shall then act as President, or the manner in which one who is to act shall be selected, and such person shall act accordingly until a President or Vice President shall have qualified.

SECTION. 4. The Congress may by law provide for the case of the death of any of the persons from whom the House of Representatives may choose a President whenever the right of choice shall have devolved upon them, and for the case of the death of any of the persons from whom the Senate may choose a Vice President whenever the right of choice shall have devolved upon them.

SECTION. 5. Sections 1 and 2 shall take effect on the 15th day of October following the ratification of this article.

SECTION. 6. This article shall be inoperative unless it shall have been ratified as an amendment to the Constitution by the legislatures of three fourths of the several States within seven years from the date of its submission.

Amendment XXI

SECTION. 1. The eighteenth article of amendment to the Constitution of the United States is hereby repealed.

SECTION. 2. The transportation or importation into any State, territory, or possession of the United States for delivery or use therein of intoxicating liquors, in violation of the laws thereof, is hereby prohibited.

SECTION. 3. This article shall be inoperative unless it shall have been ratified as an amendment to the Constitution by convention in the several States, as provided in the Constitution, within seven years from the date of the submission thereof to the States by the Congress.

Amendment XXII

SECTION. 1. No person shall be elected to the office of the President more than twice, and no person who has held the office of President, or acted as President, for more than two years of a term to which some other person was elected President shall be elected to the office of the President more than once. But this article shall not apply to any person holding the office of President when this article was proposed by the Congress, and shall not prevent any person who may be holding the office of President, or acting as President, during the term within which this article becomes operative from holding the office of President or acting as President during the remainder of such term.

SECTION. 2. This article shall be inoperative unless it shall have been ratified as an amendment to the Constitution by the legislatures of three fourths of the several States within seven years from the date of its submission to the States by the Congress.

Amendment XXIII

SECTION. 1. The District constituting the seat of Government of the United States shall appoint in such manner as the Congress may direct: A number of electors of President and Vice President equal to the whole number of Senators and Representatives in Congress to which the District would be entitled if it were a State, but in no event more than the least populous State; they shall be in addition to those appointed by the States, but they shall be considered, for the purposes of the election of President and Vice President, to be electors appointed by a State; and they shall meet in the District and perform such duties as provided by the twelfth article of amendment.

SECTION. 2. The Congress shall have the power to enforce this article by appropriate legislation.

Amendment XXIV

SECTION. 1. The right of citizens of the United States to vote in any primary or other election for President or Vice President, for electors for President or Vice President, or for Senator or Representative in Congress, shall not be denied or abridged by the United States or any State by reasons of failure to pay any poll tax or other tax.

SECTION. 2. The Congress shall have the power to enforce this article by appropriate legislation.

Amendment XXV

SECTION. 1. In case of the removal of the President from office or of his death or resignation, the Vice President shall become President.

SECTION. 2. Whenever there is a vacancy in the office of the Vice President, the President shall nominate a Vice President who shall take office upon confirmation by a majority vote of both Houses of Congress.

SECTION. 3. Whenever the President transmits to the President pro tempore of the Senate and the Speaker of the House of Representatives his written declaration that he is unable to discharge the powers and duties of his office, and until he transmits to them a written declaration to the contrary, such powers and duties shall be discharged by the Vice President as Acting President.

SECTION. 4. Whenever the Vice President and a majority of either the principal officers of the executive departments or of such other body as Congress may by law provide, transmit to the President pro tempore of the Senate and the Speaker of the House of Representatives their written declaration that the President is unable to discharge the powers and duties of his office, the Vice President shall immediately assume the powers and duties of the office as Acting President.

Thereafter, when the President transmits to the President pro tempore of the Senate and the Speaker of the House of

Representatives his written declaration that no inability exists, he shall resume the powers and duties of his office unless the Vice President and a majority of either the principal officers of the executive department or of such other body as Congress may by law provide, transmit within four days to the President pro tempore of the Senate and the Speaker of the House of Representatives their written declaration that the President is unable to discharge the powers and duties of his office. Thereupon Congress shall decide the issue, assembling within forty-eight hours for that purpose if not in session. If the Congress, within twenty-one days after receipt of the latter written declaration, or, if Congress is not in session, within twenty-one days after Congress is required to assemble, determines by two thirds vote of both Houses that the President is unable to discharge the powers and duties of his office, the Vice President shall continue to discharge the same as Acting President; otherwise, the President shall resume the powers and duties of his office.

Amendment XXVI

SECTION. 1. The right of citizens of the United States, who are 18 years of age or older, to vote shall not be denied or abridged by the United States or by any state on account of age.

SECTION. 2. The Congress shall have power to enforce this article by appropriate legislation.

Amendment XXVII

No law, varying the compensation for the services of the Senators and Representatives, shall take effect, until an election of Representatives shall have intervened.

THE UNIVERSAL DECLARATION OF HUMAN RIGHTS

G.A. res. 217A (III), U.N. Doc A/810 at 71 (1948)

PREAMBLE

Whereas recognition of the inherent dignity and of the equal and inalienable rights of all members of the human family is the foundation of freedom, justice and peace in the world,

Whereas disregard and contempt for human rights have resulted in barbarous acts which have outraged the conscience of mankind, and the advent of a world in which human beings shall enjoy freedom of speech and belief and freedom from fear and want has been proclaimed as the highest aspiration of the common people,

Whereas it is essential, if man is not to be compelled to have recourse, as a last resort, to rebellion against tyranny and oppression, that human rights should be protected by the rule of law,

Whereas it is essential to promote the development of friendly relations between nations,

Whereas the peoples of the United Nations have in the Charter reaffirmed their faith in fundamental human rights, in the dignity and worth of the human person and in the equal rights of men and women and have determined to promote social progress and better standards of life in larger freedom,

Whereas Member States have pledged themselves to achieve, in cooperation with the United Nations, the promotion of universal respect for and observance of human rights and fundamental freedoms,

Whereas a common understanding of these rights and freedoms is of the greatest importance for the full realization of this pledge,

Now, therefore,

The General Assembly,

Proclaims this Universal Declaration of Human Rights as a common standard of achievement for all peoples and all nations, to the end that every individual and every organ of society, keeping this Declaration constantly in mind, shall strive by teaching and education to promote respect for these rights and freedoms and by progressive measures, national and international, to secure their universal and effective recognition and observance, both among the peoples of Member States themselves and among the peoples of territories under their jurisdiction.

Article I

All human beings are born free and equal in dignity and rights. They are endowed with reason and conscience and should act towards one another in a spirit of brotherhood.

Article 2

Everyone is entitled to all the rights and freedoms set forth in this Declaration, without distinction of any kind, such as race, colour, sex, language, religion, political or other opinion, national or social origin, property, birth or other status.

Furthermore, no distinction shall be made on the basis of the political, jurisdictional or international status of the country or territory to which a person belongs, whether it be independent, trust, non-self-governing or under any other limitation of sovereignty.

Article 3

Everyone has the right to life, liberty and security of person.

Article 4

No one shall be held in slavery or servitude; slavery and the slave trade shall be prohibited in all their forms.

Article 5

No one shall be subjected to torture or to cruel, inhuman or degrading treatment or punishment.

Article 6

Everyone has the right to recognition everywhere as a person before the law.

Article 7

All are equal before the law and are entitled without any discrimination to equal protection of the law. All are entitled to equal protection against any discrimination in violation of this Declaration and against any incitement to such discrimination.

Article 8

Everyone has the right to an effective remedy by the competent national tribunals for acts violating the fundamental rights granted him by the constitution or by law.

Article 9

No one shall be subjected to arbitrary arrest, detention or exile.

Article 10

Everyone is entitled in full equality to a fair and public hearing by an independent and impartial tribunal, in the determination of his rights and obligations and of any criminal charge against him.

Article 11

1. Everyone charged with a penal offence has the right to be presumed innocent until proved guilty according to law in a public trial at which he has had all the guarantees necessary for his defence.

2. No one shall be held guilty of any penal offence on account of any act or omission which did not constitute a penal offence, under national or international law, at the time when it was committed. Nor shall a heavier penalty be imposed than the one that was applicable at the time the penal offence was committed.

Article 12

No one shall be subjected to arbitrary interference with his privacy, family, home or correspondence, nor to attacks upon his honour and reputation. Everyone has the right to the protection of the law against such interference or attacks.

Article 13

1. Everyone has the right to freedom of movement and residence within the borders of each State. 2. Everyone has the right to leave any country, including his own, and to return to his country.

Article 14

1. Everyone has the right to seek and to enjoy in other countries asylum from persecution.

2. This right may not be invoked in the case of prosecutions genuinely arising from non-political crimes or from acts contrary to the purposes and principles of the United Nations.

Article 15

1. Everyone has the right to a nationality.

2. No one shall be arbitrarily deprived of his nationality nor denied the right to change his nationality.

Article 16

1. Men and women of full age, without any limitation due to race, nationality or religion, have the right to marry and to found a family. They are entitled to equal rights as to marriage, during marriage and at its dissolution.

2. Marriage shall be entered into only with the free and full consent of the intending spouses.

3. The family is the natural and fundamental group unit of society and is entitled to protection by society and the State.

Article 17

1. Everyone has the right to own property alone as well as in association with others.

2. No one shall be arbitrarily deprived of his property.

Article 18

Everyone has the right to freedom of thought, conscience and religion; this right includes freedom to change his religion or belief, and freedom, either alone or in community with others and in public or private, to manifest his religion or belief in teaching, practice, worship and observance.

Article 19

Everyone has the right to freedom of opinion and expression; this right includes freedom to hold opinions without interference and to seek, receive and impart information and ideas through any media and regardless of frontiers.

Article 20

1. Everyone has the right to freedom of peaceful assembly and association.

2. No one may be compelled to belong to an association.

Article 21

1. Everyone has the right to take part in the government of his country, directly or through freely chosen representatives.

2. Everyone has the right to equal access to public service in his country.

3. The will of the people shall be the basis of the authority of government; this will shall be expressed in periodic and genuine elections which shall be by universal and equal suffrage and shall be held by secret vote or by equivalent free voting procedures.

Article 22

Everyone, as a member of society, has the right to social security and is entitled to realization, through national effort and international co-operation and in accordance with the organization and resources of each State, of the economic, social and cultural rights indispensable for his dignity and the free development of his personality.

Article 23

1. Everyone has the right to work, to free choice of employment, to just and favourable conditions of work and to protection against unemployment.

2. Everyone, without any discrimination, has the right to equal pay for equal work.

3. Everyone who works has the right to just and favourable remuneration ensuring for himself and his family an existence worthy of human dignity, and supplemented, if necessary, by other means of social protection.

4. Everyone has the right to form and to join trade unions for the protection of his interests.

Article 24

Everyone has the right to rest and leisure, including reasonable limitation of working hours and periodic holidays with pay.

Article 25

1. Everyone has the right to a standard of living adequate for the health and well-being of himself and of his family, including food, clothing, housing and medical care and necessary social services, and the right to security in the event of unemployment, sickness, disability, widowhood, old age or other lack of livelihood in circumstances beyond his control.

2. Motherhood and childhood are entitled to special care and assistance. All children, whether born in or out of wedlock, shall enjoy the same social protection.

Article 26

1. Everyone has the right to education. Education shall be free, at least in the elementary and fundamental stages. Elementary education shall be compulsory. Technical and professional education shall be made generally available and higher education shall be equally accessible to all on the basis of merit.

2. Education shall be directed to the full development of the human personality and to the strengthening of respect for human rights and fundamental freedoms. It shall promote understanding, tolerance and friendship among all nations, racial or religious groups, and shall further the activities of the United Nations for the maintenance of peace.

3. Parents have a prior right to choose the kind of education that shall be given to their children.

Article 27

1. Everyone has the right freely to participate in the cultural life of the community, to enjoy the arts and to share in scientific advancement and its benefits.

2. Everyone has the right to the protection of the moral and material interests resulting from any scientific, literary or artistic production of which he is the author.

Article 28

Everyone is entitled to a social and international order in which the rights and freedoms set forth in this Declaration can be fully realized.

Article 29

1. Everyone has duties to the community in which alone the free and full development of his personality is possible.

2. In the exercise of his rights and freedoms, everyone shall be subject only to such limitations as are determined by law solely for the purpose of securing due recognition and respect for the rights and freedoms of others and of meeting the just requirements of morality, public order and the general welfare in a democratic society.

3. These rights and freedoms may in no case be exercised contrary to the purposes and principles of the United Nations.

Article 30

Nothing in this Declaration may be interpreted as implying for any State, group or person any right to engage in any activity or to perform any act aimed at the destruction of any of the rights and freedoms set forth herein.

THE CAIRO DECLARATION ON HUMAN RIGHTS IN ISLAM

Adopted and Issued at the Nineteenth Islamic Conference of Foreign Ministers in Cairo on 5 August 1990.

The Member States of the Organization of the Islamic Conference,[393]

Reaffirming the civilizing and historical role of the Islamic Ummah which God made the best nation that has given mankind a universal and well-balanced civilization in which harmony is established between this life and the hereafter and knowledge is combined with faith; and the role that this Ummah should play to guide a humanity confused by competing trends and ideologies and to provide solutions to the chronic problems of this materialistic civilization.

Wishing to contribute to the efforts of mankind to assert human rights, to protect man from exploitation and persecution, and to affirm his freedom and right to a dignified life in accordance with the Islamic Shari'ah

Convinced that mankind which has reached an advanced stage in materialistic science is still, and shall remain, in dire need of faith to support its civilization and of a self-motivating force to guard its rights;

Believing that fundamental rights and universal freedoms in Islam are an integral part of the Islamic religion and that no one as a matter of principle has the right to suspend them in whole or in part or violate or ignore them in as much as they are binding

---

393 As noted previously, the Organization of the Islamic Conference changed its name in 2011 to the Organization of Islamic Cooperation.

divine commandments, which are contained in the Revealed Books of God and were sent through the last of His Prophets to complete the preceding divine messages thereby making their observance an act of worship and their neglect or violation an abominable sin, and accordingly every person is individually responsible — and the Ummah collectively responsible — for their safeguard.

Proceeding from the above-mentioned principles,

Declare the following:

Article 1

(a) All human beings form one family whose members are united by submission to God and descent from Adam. All men are equal in terms of basic human dignity and basic obligations and responsibilities, without any discrimination on the grounds of race, colour, language, sex, religious belief, political affiliation, social status or other considerations. True faith is the guarantee for enhancing such dignity along the path to human perfection.

(b) All human beings are God's subjects, and the most loved by him are those who are most useful to the rest of His subjects, and no one has superiority over another except on the basis of piety and good deeds.

Article 2

(a) Life is a God-given gift and the right to life is guaranteed to every human being. It is the duty of individuals, societies and states to protect this right from any violation, and it is prohibited to take away life except for a Shari'ah-prescribed reason.

(b) It is forbidden to resort to such means as may result in the genocidal annihilation of mankind.

(c) The preservation of human life throughout the term of time willed by God is a duty prescribed by Shari'ah.

(d) Safety from bodily harm is a guaranteed right. It is the duty of the state to safeguard it, and it is prohibited to breach it without a Shari'ah-prescribed reason.

Article 3

(a) In the event of the use of force and in case of armed conflict, it is not permissible to kill non-belligerents such as old men, women and children. The wounded and the sick shall have the right to medical treatment; and prisoners of war shall have the right to be fed, sheltered and clothed. It is prohibited to mutilate dead bodies. It is a duty to exchange prisoners of war and to arrange visits or reunions of the families separated by the circumstances of war.

(b) It is prohibited to fell trees, to damage crops or livestock, and to destroy the enemy's civilian buildings and installations by shelling, blasting or any other means.

Article 4

Every human being is entitled to inviolability and the protection of his good name and honour during his life and after his death. The state and society shall protect his remains and burial place.

Article 5

(a) The family is the foundation of society, and marriage is the basis of its formation. Men and women have the right to marriage, and no restrictions stemming from race, colour or nationality shall prevent them from enjoying this right.

(b) Society and the State shall remove all obstacles to marriage and shall facilitate marital procedure. They shall ensure family protection and welfare.

Article 6

(a) Woman is equal to man in human dignity, and has rights to enjoy as well as duties to perform; she has her own civil entity and financial independence, and the right to retain her name and lineage.

(b) The husband is responsible for the support and welfare of the family.

Article 7

(a) As of the moment of birth, every child has rights due from the parents, society and the state to be accorded proper nursing, education and material, hygienic and moral care. Both the fetus and the mother must be protected and accorded special care.

(b) Parents and those in such like capacity have the right to choose the type of education they desire for their children, provided they take into consideration the interest and future of the children in accordance with ethical values and the principles of the Shari'ah.

(c) Both parents are entitled to certain rights from their children, and relatives are entitled to rights from their kin, in accordance with the tenets of the Shari'ah.

Article 8

Every human being has the right to enjoy his legal capacity in terms of both obligation and commitment. Should this capacity be lost or impaired, he shall be represented by his guardian.

Article 9

(a) The quest for knowledge is an obligation, and the provision of education is a duty for society and the State. The State shall ensure the availability of ways and means to acquire education and shall guarantee educational diversity in the interest of society so as to enable man to be acquainted with the religion of Islam and the facts of the Universe for the benefit of mankind.

(b) Every human being has the right to receive both religious and worldly education from the various institutions of education and guidance, including the family, the school, the university, the media, etc., and in such an integrated and balanced manner as to develop his personality, strengthen his faith in God and promote his respect for and defence of both rights and obligations.

Article 10

Islam is the religion of unspoiled nature. It is prohibited to exercise any form of compulsion on man or to exploit his poverty or ignorance in order to convert him to another religion or to atheism.

Article 11

(a) Human beings are born free, and no one has the right to enslave, humiliate, oppress or exploit them, and there can be no subjugation but to God the Most-High.

(b) Colonialism of all types being one of the most evil forms of enslavement is totally prohibited. Peoples suffering from colonialism have the full right to freedom and self-determination. It is the duty of all States and peoples to support the struggle of colonized peoples for the liquidation of all forms of colonialism and occupation, and all States and peoples have the right to preserve their independent identity and exercise control over their wealth and natural resources.

Article 12

Every man shall have the right, within the framework of Shari'ah, to free movement and to select his place of residence whether inside or outside his country and, if persecuted, is entitled to seek asylum in another country. The country of refuge shall ensure his protection until he reaches safety, unless asylum is motivated by an act which Shari'ah regards as a crime.

Article 13

Work is a right guaranteed by the State and Society for each person able to work. Everyone shall be free to choose the work that suits him best and which serves his interests and those of society. The employee shall have the right to safety and security as well as to all other social guarantees. He may neither be assigned work beyond his capacity nor be subjected to compulsion or exploited or harmed in any way. He shall be entitled — without any discrimination between males and females — to fair wages for his work without delay, as well as to the holidays, allowances and promotions which he deserves. For his part, he shall be required to be dedicated and meticulous in his work. Should workers and employers disagree on any matter, the State shall intervene to settle the dispute and have the grievances redressed, the rights confirmed and justice enforced without bias.

Article 14

Everyone shall have the right to legitimate gains without monopolization, deceit or harm to oneself or to others. Usury (riba) is absolutely prohibited.

Article 15

(a) Everyone shall have the right to own property acquired in a legitimate way, and shall be entitled to the rights of ownership, without prejudice to oneself, others or to society in general. Expropriation is not permissible except for the requirements of public interest and upon payment of immediate and fair compensation

(b) Confiscation and seizure of property is prohibited except for a necessity dictated by law.

Article 16

Everyone shall have the right to enjoy the fruits of his scientific, literary, artistic or technical production and the right to protect the moral and material interests stemming therefrom, provided that such production is not contrary to the principles of Shari'ah.

Article 17

(a) Everyone shall have the right to live in a clean environment, away from vice and moral corruption, an environment that would foster his self-development; and it is incumbent upon the State and society in general to afford that right.

(b) Everyone shall have the right to medical and social care, and to all public amenities provided by society and the State within the limits of their available resources.

(c) The State shall ensure the right of the individual to a decent living which will enable him to meet all his requirements and those of his dependents, including food, clothing, housing, education, medical care and all other basic needs.

Article 18

(a) Everyone shall have the right to live in security for himself, his religion, his dependents, his honour and his property.

(b) Everyone shall have the right to privacy in the conduct of his private affairs, in his home, among his family, with regard to his property and his relationships. It is not permitted to spy on him, to place him under surveillance or to besmirch his good name. The State shall protect him from arbitrary interference.

(c) A private residence is inviolable in all cases. It will not be entered without permission from its inhabitants or in any unlawful manner, nor shall it be demolished or confiscated and its dwellers evicted.

Article 19

(a) All individuals are equal before the law, without distinction between the ruler and the ruled.

(b) The right to resort to justice is guaranteed to everyone.

(c) Liability is in essence personal.

(d) There shall be no crime or punishment except as provided for in the Shari'ah.

(e) A defendant is innocent until his guilt is proven in a fair trial in which he shall be given all the guarantees of defence.

Article 20

It is not permitted without legitimate reason to arrest an individual, or restrict his freedom, to exile or to punish him. It is not permitted to subject him to physical or psychological torture or to any form of humiliation, cruelty or indignity. Nor is it permitted to subject an individual to medical or scientific experimentation without his consent or at the risk of his health or of his life. Nor is it permitted to promulgate emergency laws that would provide executive authority for such actions.

Article 21

Taking hostages under any form or for any purpose is expressly forbidden.

Article 22

(a) Everyone shall have the right to express his opinion freely in such manner as would not be contrary to the principles of the Shari'ah.

(b) Everyone shall have the right to advocate what is right, and propagate what is good, and warn against what is wrong and evil according to the norms of Islamic Shari'ah.

(c) Information is a vital necessity to society. It may not be exploited or misused in such a way as may violate sanctities and the dignity of Prophets, undermine moral and ethical values or disintegrate, corrupt or harm society or weaken its faith.

(d) It is not permitted to arouse nationalistic or doctrinal hatred or to do anything that may be an incitement to any form of racial discrimination.

Article 23

(a) Authority is a trust; and abuse or malicious exploitation thereof is absolutely prohibited, so that fundamental human rights may be guaranteed.

(b) Everyone shall have the right to participate, directly or indirectly in the administration of his country's public affairs. He shall also have the right to assume public office in accordance with the provisions of Shari'ah.

Article 24

All the rights and freedoms stipulated in this Declaration are subject to the Islamic Shari'ah.

Article 25

The Islamic Shari'ah is the only source of reference for the explanation or clarification to any of the articles of this Declaration.

Cairo, 14 Muharram 1411H 5 August 1990

Made in the USA
Charleston, SC
17 June 2012